A special thank you also goes out to **Kim and Blair Chapman, Dr. Roger Neil** and **Dr. Cam Symons** for helping me through the revision process. Thank you to **Dr. Sherri-Lynn Skwarchuk, the Life Skills Class Students, staff of the Beautiful Plains School Division,** and my many **friends**—old and new—for encouraging and supporting me in getting my book published. Thank you!

Author **Kimberley Smith** is available to speak at in-services, meetings, conferences, etc. about her experiences as a sibling of a child with special needs. Her presentation would involve issues surrounding siblings and how teachers and professionals can best help this population. To reach her phone 1-204-476-5871, write Box 1382, Neepawa, MB, R0J 1H0, Canada, email kimsmith@mts.net or visit her website: www.publishedauthors.net/thelovewithinasmile/index.html

THE LOVE WITHIN HIS SMILE

He was silenced by fate,
but for me it was a blessing in disguise.
His being in my life has given me
a different outlook on life.
Without him I wouldn't know how to
be thankful for what I have.
He's taught me the value of love,
for I've learned that silence has no bearing.
I've learned not to be judgemental,
because everyone is special in their own way.
He is the most important person in my life.
I know his love will never stop
whether he's here on earth or up in heaven,
because when I need someone,
He'll always be there with a tiny gesture
that brightens my world.
He may be silenced by fate,
but that simple gesture expresses
more than words every could.
You see there is pure
"love within his smile."

March 1, 1992

TABLE OF CONTENTS

Chapter 1	11
Chapter 2	18
Chapter 3	23
Chapter 4	29
Chapter 5	34
Chapter 6	38
Chapter 7	45
Chapter 8	52
Chapter 9	58
Pictures	62
Chapter 10	77
Chapter 11	85
Chapter 12	93
Chapter 13	100
Chapter 14	106
Chapter 15	114
Chapter 16	121
Chapter 17	128
Chapter 18	140
Chapter 19	145
Supporting Siblings: A Literature Review	152
Tips for Parents	163
Tips for Professionals	167
Tips for Siblings	169
Resources for Parents, Professionals and Siblings	171
Special Education Glossary	179
References	189

CHAPTER 1

Every life has a story that should be told, so that perhaps others can better learn to appreciate what they themselves have. Fragments of my brother Mark's story have been told to many people throughout the years. Dad always tells the humorous stories of Mark's life while Mom shares the practical stories: together helping us be more aware of the lighter side of life, the challenges and the accomplishments our family faced. Twenty-three year old Trent, on the rare occasion that he enchants us with his memories, recalls the stories of Mark's personality. I tell the stories of Mark's spirit and courage and the valuable life lessons he taught us. I have told many of Mark's stories over the years to everyone I come into contact with. Many of our closest friends know much of the whole story and have been there for us as it unfolded. However, no one will truly understand Mark's journey until they listen to his story.

I don't remember the day my brother Mark was born, or the day my parents brought him home from the hospital, but in that moment my family's life changed forever. Mark Douglas Leslie was born on Wednesday, March 23, 1977 at 4:59AM. He weighed 6 lbs 8 oz. and was 22" long. Dad said that it seemed to have taken Mark hours to arrive because of the length of his body. When Mark arrived, the nurses and doctor said very little. At the time, Mom and Dad didn't think this was strange, but as they look back now, they realize this was probably their first sign of problems. Mark was born with brown hair and brown eyes that seemed to speak to your soul. His eyes always twinkled as if he had a great secret. He was long and skinny with a rather malnourished look about him. He looked as if he wasn't getting enough nutrients while in the womb. He had a very small head and webbed feet with missing toes. He had low set thumbs on both hands and had typhosis of his back with prominent vertebral spines. In other words, his spine stuck out and every single bone could be seen. My parents had a feeling that Mark was going to be different, but they had no idea just how much.

During the first few months of Mark's life, Mom and Dad noticed that he didn't seem to be progressing at the same pace as I had. He couldn't hold his head up, and everything about him just seemed to move at a slower rate. He wasn't following any objects with his eyes. At first, everyone thought that maybe he was blind, because he couldn't follow things, but they weren't sure. He could grasp items, but didn't reach for them. He didn't hold his bottle or transfer things from hand to hand. He couldn't sit up and had poor neck control. He couldn't chew or finger his food. One thing he could do though was smile! He had an incredible smile that melted your heart.

By the time Mark was a couple of months old, my Uncle Gary, who was a doctor in Winnipeg, Manitoba, had also noticed the differences in Mark and felt that my parents should see a specialist to figure out the problem. He set up an appointment in July of 1977 with specialist doctors at the Child Development Clinic in Winnipeg, so our family set off to Winnipeg to get to the bottom of the problem. We were in the city for two weeks travelling back and forth to the hospital so that the doctors could administer all sorts of tests. They did audiology (hearing) tests, vision tests, fine and gross motor (big and small muscles) tests, medical tests, etc. Finally at the end of the two weeks they diagnosed Mark as being mentally retarded, a term that brought a lot of questions, pain, and disappointment. The doctor was very pessimistic about Mark's functioning level. He told my parents that Mark would never walk or talk. He would take a lot of care and he would more than likely be very hard to handle due to his many developmental problems. He felt that my parents did not have the skills necessary to raise someone of his functioning level. He suggested that my parents put him in an institution and forget that he even existed.

According to the American Association on Mental Retardation (1992), "Mental retardation refers to substantial limitations in present functioning. It is characterized by significantly subaverage intellectual functioning, existing concurrently with related limitations in two or more of the following applicable adaptive skill areas: communication, self-care, home living, social skills, community use, self-direction, health and safety, functional academics, leisure and work. Mental retardation manifests before age 18." In general terms, a person who is mentally retarded is someone who has trouble learning as normal people do to the extent that it affects every aspect of their life. There are different levels of severity with this condition that range from mild problems to profound difficulties. Children, when they reach school age, are generally given intelligence tests such as the Stanford-Binet Intelligence Scales or the Wechsler Intelligence Scales to see where they are functioning. An IQ (intelligence quotient) of 70 or below is considered to be in the mentally retarded range. Mark, therefore, was labelled "mentally retarded" because of his low scores on the tests the doctors administered.

If Mark had been diagnosed today, they would have labelled him either developmentally delayed or at-risk. There is a stigmatism that is attached to the term "mentally retarded" and the professional world has chosen not to use this term so that the child is given a fair chance in the learning world. At-risk children are those who are at-risk for having a disability due to environmental conditions or things that happened prior to, during, or directly after birth. Developmentally delayed children are the ones who have an obvious delay. In school settings, terms like educable mental handicap (EMH), trainable mental handicap (TMH), and severe mental handicap (SMH) are used frequently to describe those students.

EMH students usually are very mild in their disability and can, with a variety of supports, function relatively well. TMH and SMH students are more severely delayed and need lots of guidance and support to function in a school or community setting. (Mark would have been considered an SMH student). Generally, these individuals will forever need assistance in their lives. Other terms that are used today are mentally challenged, mentally disabled, and mentally handicapped.

The term mentally retarded is one that I refuse to use. I think growing up with a brother who was classified this way is the reason why. This term caused a lot of teasing when I was younger as I will explain later on. Most people also use this term in a very negative way without even realizing it. Throughout my school years, I used to make a big fuss if anyone used this term around me in a negative way. I have learned throughout my years, that I would be causing fights wherever I go, so I have refrained from expressing my disgust about this to people I don't know well. Those closest to me know not to use this term. I use many terms when I talk about my brother and in my professional world as a special educator, but the one thing that I always do is talk about the person first and then the disability. Every individual is a person with a unique personality and they deserve the recognition first before the disability.

I think this whole world is filled with labels and our behaviours reinforce these labels everyday. When a child gets a label, it's as if the child does everything in their power to live up to the label. People seem to treat the child according to the label rather than treating them as normally as possible. A lot of times I think the world (and I don't just mean the professional world) has stopped seeing people as people. So many people focus on the label first and then they set limitations in their minds for what that person is capable of doing. Such labelling of a child is very frightening for parents. Often, the parents are in denial even though they realize that something is seriously wrong.

Even after the doctor told my parents the devastating news, they refused to listen to his suggestions. They walked out of that office and never looked back. As my Mom always says, they just forgot everything the doctor said and went home to raise their son the best way they could. I always ask them why they made that decision or if they ever had any doubt or even what was going through their heads. Mom said there was no decision to make. They brought him into this world and it was their responsibility to look after him. Neither Mark nor I realized at that time what wonderful parents we had, but as I look back now I don't know how I could ever have thought differently. A lot of people couldn't have done what they did, and yet, a lot have done the very same thing. To this day I wish I could find that doctor and show him how truly wrong he was. Some days I can't believe how a doctor could actually think that the best place for anyone would be in an institution rather than a loving home. Other days I feel sorry for people who still have such narrow outlooks.

At that time and maybe even still today, some didn't understand that people with disabilities can lead fulfilling lives. They just need someone to care. In the 1970's people were just starting to realize the capabilities of people with disabilities. Before this, people with disabilities were being shoved off to institutions or were brought up behind closed doors. In the United States, a 1971 court case in Pennsylvania (Pennsylvania Association for Retarded Children v. Commonwealth of Pennsylvania) and a 1972 court case in Washington, D.C. (Mills v. Board of Education of the District of Columbia) started the movement for students with disabilities to be educated in the public school setting. Before this public schooling was never even considered for people with disabilities.

In 1973 the Rehabilitation Act (Section 504) was passed in the United States. This civil rights law stated that people with disabilities should have the same rights as non-disabled people including any aids, benefits, or services that all people are entitled to. It wasn't until Public Law 94-142, Education for All Handicapped Children Act, was passed in 1975 that students with disabilities were guaranteed the right to a "free, appropriate public education." This law became a benchmark for all schools when providing services to students with disabilities. This law stated that no child could be refused an education. Amazing things started to happen for people with disabilities as a result of these new laws. They were now being recognized as valuable and educable human beings. It was just the start of a battle that still, to some degree, exists in schools and the world today. Thankfully, today there are many more laws that protect the freedom and rights of all individuals with disabilities. However, laws cannot legislate compassion. The laws meant that people had something to give them leverage, but people's opinions still interfered.

Mom and Dad were never given a reason to explain why Mark was the way he was. The only reason that doctors thought was a possibility was the size of his head. Mark had a small head circumference when he was born. It was only 12 inches or 30 centimetres, which is very small. This is called microcephaly or abnormal smallness of the head. The doctors thought that this could have been because of genetics due to the fact that both my parents have rather small heads.

My parents, however, have thought of a variety of other possibilities, all of which are just speculation. Virden is known as the oil capital of Manitoba, and for good reason. There are lots of drilling rigs, service rigs and oil batteries all around the Virden area. Behind our house lies an oil battery. My parents often wondered if the hydrogen sulphide gas in the air was bad for Mom's health while she was pregnant or if there were more pollutants in our water because of the oil. Mom also painted parts of our house when she was pregnant with Mark. She remembers being in a closet painting for the majority of one day. Those dangerous paint fumes could also have caused Mark's problems as doctors nowadays stress not to paint during pregnancy. Mark was also conceived during spraying season. Dad was busy spraying his fields with dangerous chemicals to help kill the weeds. My parents have wondered if Dad got any of those chemicals on him before Mark was conceived. Another possibility revolved around me.

Guilt is a common emotion for siblings of children with disabilities (or SIBS as referred to by the literature). Often they feel guilty for not being disabled themselves or they have the perception that they may have caused their sibling to be disabled. This was a perception that I had when I was young. From pieces of conversations that my parents had, I wondered if I was the cause of Mark's disabilities. When Mom was 6 months pregnant with Mark, I was about 1 1/2 years old. I always liked to be upside down or jumping around in the air—a hint of the figure skater coming out in me. Well, as Dad says, I pulled one of my stunts again and fell off something. Everyone thought I had broken my wrist. I cried and cried because it hurt so much. Mom took me to the doctor for an x-ray. I was, and still am, a very shy person who was petrified of new things and people and I'm sure I would have wanted Mom to come with me. Mom doesn't remember if she came in with me or, if she did, if they even covered her up. No one really remembers the events that took place that day and as a child, it made me wonder if things could have been different. I now know that x-rays give off a low amount of radiation that doesn't usually cause any problems, but x-ray technicians still make sure they cover pregnant women. I no longer feel guilty about Mark's disability, but while I was young it was something that plagued me.

    My faith has made me realize that everything happens for a reason. I now believe that Mark's disability was simply fate. Over the years, I have realized that I wouldn't be the person I am today if Mark wasn't the way he was. In that way I am thankful for the gifts my brother has given me. I truly believe that Mark was sent to earth to show us the miracle of life and I was sent to help people see the human spirit within that miracle.

CHAPTER 2

Once a child is diagnosed as having a disability, a team of professionals is usually notified to provide assistance to the family. A Community Service Worker (CSW) works through Children's Special Services throughout Manitoba. They provide a variety of supports to families to help care for children with disabilities under 17 years of age. Special Services provides parents with counselling to help deal with their child. It gives parents information and will referral them to other needed services. Respite care (when a qualified worker comes into your home to look after your child so you can have a break or spend time with your other children) is also provided. Through child development, the community service worker will help create a program for the parents to work on with their child. Therapy services such as occupational therapy, physiotherapy, speech and language, behavioural or developmental therapy can be provided depending on the child's needs. Children's Special Services can also provide special equipment, supplies such as special diapers, help to make necessary home design changes, transportation to medical appointments and more training to help parents raise their children. (These services are provided today, but the services may have been different back in the 1970's.)

In Mark's case, a Community Service Worker and a Behaviour

Counsellor were assigned to help my parents around his first birthday. He was placed on an individual plan to help teach him a variety of skills. This plan was an individual family service plan (IFSP). It is generally written for children with special needs from birth to 5 years of age. It focuses on the services and supports for the entire family, although I don't know many that focus on the needs of the siblings. It usually contains a statement about the child's level of physical, cognitive, communicative, social/emotional and adaptive development. It also contains the major goals for the child, the services the family needs, a transition plan for when the child reaches kindergarten and the name of the community service worker.

There are many skills that people know how to do that they take for granted every day. When it comes to people with mental disabilities, every skill has to be taught and repeated time and again until the skill has been mastered. Some of these skills may never be learned while others take years to learn. In December of 1977, the Community Service Worker and Behaviour Counsellor observed Mark at home and decided that Mark needed to be placed in the Infant Stimulation and Developmental Training program. The Behaviour Counsellor designed the program with input from my mom. Mom would then run the program using all the suggestions from the counsellor. My mom had to take data on all the behaviours that she was teaching as well as on any new behaviour that Mark did. Mom also took a behaviour modification course to help out with Mark's learning. Examples of some of the behaviours that Mom had to teach Mark were transferring objects from one hand to another, holding an object in both hands, standing with support for a minute, following with his eyes as someone walked around, picking up a cookie, putting a cookie to his mouth, rolling over, and looking when his name was called. Mom and the Behaviour Counsellor went to great lengths to teach Mark how to do some of these simple things. They had to come up with inventive ways of teaching a simple task so that Mark could learn how to do it. For example they used a cardboard box to teach him how to sit up. They sat Mark in a box with full support up to his neck. Mom did this for a certain amount of time each day. As the days went on, she gradually cut the box down so that there was less support for him. Finally in September of 1978 when he was 18 months old, Mark learned how to sit up independently. It was a great accomplishment.

Every behaviour that Mark was taught had to be completely dissected down into tiny steps. This is called a task analysis. A task analysis is written for any task so that when teaching the child you can see where they are having difficulty. Below is a task analysis that was used to teach Mark how to sit on his knees. Mom had to perform this task two to three times a day for many months, and to be honest, I don't remember him ever being able to do it.

Task Analysis for Knee Sitting:
Step 1: Sit on the ground.
Step 2: Move one leg underneath you by swinging it around and putting your arm on the ground for support.
Step 3: Move your other leg underneath you in the same way.
Step 4: Sit up straight.

Task Analysis for Mom to Teach the Skill:
Step 1: Place Mark on his knees with his one side against the wall.
Step 2: Place your hand on the other side for support.
Step 3: If he sits for 5 seconds, lie him down and give him a toy.
Step 4: When he does this consistently (5 consecutive times) increase it to 10 seconds.

I have created task analyses that have involved 50 steps. It can be difficult to break down a skill into individual parts for very simple tasks, but it is essential to create a task analysis for everything that is taught to a person with a mental disability.

Mom spent the majority of her days working with Mark. I don't really remember what I did, but Mom said that I was always trying to help out in any way that I could. From the time Mark came along, she knew my career choice would be teaching. To this day I have no idea what I would have done if I hadn't chosen to become a teacher.

Research says that it is quite common for siblings of people with disabilities to enter into related fields because of their childhood experiences.

There were a lot of adjustments that everyone in our family had to make. Mine was probably the easiest as I was only two years old and had never really lived life without a brother with a disability. I actually never understood that Mark was so different until I was in school. I thought every family had someone like him. I knew my new brother needed lots of attention so I just accepted that. As I grew up, however, there were times that this bothered me. It's often difficult for siblings, either older or younger, to realize that the child with special needs requires an enormous amount of attention. I think it's important for parents to realize that siblings often can feel left out or not important. Parents need to spend one-on-one time with all their children. I don't remember my parents ever explaining Mark's disability to me, but it is important for parents to take the extra time to explain the situation.

My parents did a great job of helping me adjust, but it was their lives that required the most sacrifices. Before Mark and I came along, my parents were very busy living life to its fullest. Dad played hockey a couple of nights a week in Miniota, MB as well as spent time with his friends frequently. In the summer, Dad was busy becoming the farmer that he is today. Mom worked as a secretary at the Chevron office in Virden. She enjoyed her curling and went to bonspiels almost every weekend. They spent countless hours with their family and friends, but all that changed when Mark was born. There wasn't time for all the extra-curricular activities because Mark's needs were so great. There were always trips to hospitals, medical clinics, special devices clinics, and the list just went on and on and on. They had to rearrange everything in their life and learn to accept Mark's disability. Numerous authors state that parents go through a type of "mourning period" when faced with a child with a disability. When parents are expecting a baby, it is only natural to dream of what your child is going to be when they grow up. You think of all the wonderful things you are going to teach your child and times that you are going to spend together. You have their whole life planned out before they're even born. Of course, it never is the way you imagine it, but no one ever thinks that some of these dreams just are not possible until the day that their child is diagnosed as having a disability. There is an essay called "Welcome to Holland" by Emily Perl Kingsley that explains this time in a parents' life better than I ever could.

Parents go through several stages before they accept their child's new identity. Guilt, denial, depression, and anger are just a few of these stages. Not all families go through this, but it is a normal process. It has been described as being very similar to the grief process of losing a child. Parents must learn to accept their child and move on in order to help them. Unfortunately, some families never do reach this stage and deal with this mourning process their whole lives. Even though my parents don't admit it, they went through this process themselves. Mom said the first few years were very difficult. They had to learn to cope with what God gave them. Not only did they have to cope themselves, but they also had to deal with what others thought, and this was probably the toughest for them. Certain friends didn't visit as much as before and others didn't ask about Mark like they would about a normal child. Some people in the community also brought pain to our family by not accepting Mark or ignoring him. Dad spent a lot of time in the field or working in his shop those first few years. I guess that was his way of dealing with it. Mom said she just had to accept it and move on because there were things that she needed to do to help Mark. Luckily for us, we had great family and wonderful friends to provide us with support.

One friend in fact found a poem entitled "Heaven's Very Special Child" by Edna Massimilla in a newspaper and gave it to Mom. Mom said the poem helped her see the beauty in her angel from God.

CHAPTER 3

I have met a lot of wonderful men in my life—grandfathers, uncles, cousins, friends, brothers, and my husband—but the man that I consider the greatest is the one to which I compare all others. My father was the first man I met and the first to love me. My Dad can come off as being a tough, grumpy guy, but when you see through to his soul you will find a very compassionate and loving man. As we grew up, it was Dad's deep stern voice that we were scared of because we knew we were in big trouble if he was involved. The thing about my Dad, however, was that no matter how serious the problem, he made us find the humour in the situation. His laughter always filled our home. We couldn't stay mad at anyone for long because he bugged us until he found our smile. Dad loved to tease. You knew if he liked someone by how much he teased him or her. Before we were born, Dad would tease Mom so much that she would end up in tears. Dad never wants to hurt anyone, but he sometimes doesn't stop until he has got you steaming! Mom said she was glad when we came along because he turned his talent on us. There was always something he could find to tease about. With me it was always easy. I cry at the drop of a hat. Trent was a lot harder to tease. He would just get mad and leave the room. Mark's teasing was different. It was the kind of teasing that you give to babies. It had a little extra love and gentleness to it.

Dad always made us strive to do the best we could. He had very high expectations for us and I think that is probably why we all accomplished so much. He would never let us quit. He thought quitting was a sign of weakness. It was the coward's way out. I would have to say that is something I am thankful for. I wouldn't have been able to write this book, Mark may never have walked, and Trent may have just given up on life completely. I would come home with B's and Dad would ask why they weren't A's. I would come home from a piano exam passing with honours. He would tell me that I must have screwed up a song. A lot of times this made me angry because I felt like I was never good enough. Sometimes I thought that maybe he was trying to get me to make up for Mark's limitations, but I think he pushed us because he knew we were capable of doing more than we thought we could. It frustrated all three of us at one point or another, but now that we reflect on Mark's life we know that his way of teaching us helped us overcome some of our greatest challenges.

Dad is an amazing storyteller. In fact, it should be him writing this story rather than me. He has a unique way of telling stories. All conversations stop and everyone's focus turns to the story that he is telling. His tone of voice makes you sit on the edge of your seat until you are bursting! He can bring you to tears one minute and have you laughing hysterically the next. Dad also enjoys having stories told to him through various forms—books, history, movies, and music. According to him you have not lived until you have seen "Gone With The Wind" or watched a movie with the great American hero, John Wayne. Until you let the music of Patsy Cline or Buddy Holly capture your soul, you are not complete. History repeats itself and so he feels compelled to share his love of the past—famous or not. A western book, a biography of someone who has shaped our world, or a book about his favourite sport, hockey, are never far from his sight. He feels that reading a good book can teach you more than any class at school. Throughout all his stories we found the life lessons that have shaped our values.

He wasn't one to say that he loved us or tell us he was proud. Hugs and kisses were not common, but given when truly needed. His actions held the emotions. Whether it was to get off a tractor to take a child to a practice or break a commitment to stay home to look after an ailing child, he was always there for us. He showed us the power of love in all he did.

With Mark's needs came appointments after appointments. Many of these appointments were only attended by Mom, but Dad's support was there in spirit. Dad would always go to the appointments out of town. An example of these appointments was our visits to the Special Devices Clinic at the Shriners Hospital in Winnipeg. Our family went there frequently to borrow special equipment to assist Mark with his physical challenges. He had many kinds of special equipment over the years. To start with, he had a floor seat that helped him learn how to sit up. He had a floor crawler, a bath seat, special spoons to eat with, and a standing frame/table as well as many wheelchairs and walkers.

Home visits continued throughout Mark's preschool years. Generally these visits were Mom's responsibility as Dad was working. These visits included many people such as a physiotherapist, the community service worker, and the behaviour counsellor. Evaluations of the programs occurred frequently. Gradually the home visits were faded out and replaced by phone calls. Different areas that Mom concentrated on teaching Mark were moving from sitting to lying, lying to sitting, and spoon-feeding. Mom had to continue these sessions three times a day and record data of all Mark's behaviours. Data collection is very important when teaching children with disabilities a new task. It can range from any kind of test to observation to interviewing those involved. Data often shows where problem areas lie as well as providing some solutions to those areas. As a special educator, I use data collection every day in different ways for different tasks.

There are also many different techniques to teaching children a task. Some times it can be referred to as shaping behaviour. Forward chaining, for example, is used to link tiny steps together until you have the whole skill mastered. With this process, you start with the first little step and work your way through to the final step of the task.

Backward chaining is the exact opposite. You start with the last step and work towards the first step. Within these techniques, a system of prompts assists the teaching process. A teacher can provide a verbal prompt, a gesture, and a physical prompt or can model the behaviour for a student. Just one or all of those prompts can be used depending on the need of the student. A task is sometimes too difficult for students with severe disabilities to complete on their own. Sometimes they may only be able to do certain steps. It is known as partial participation when the student does half the steps and someone else does the rest. Students with disabilities need to work towards independence, but sometimes assistance is necessary.

For children with severe disabilities such as my brother's, one must think the whole teaching process out carefully by considering the task, the technique to use, data collection, prompts and the reinforcers that are needed. Because these types of children learn so slowly, it is important to pay careful attention to every detail. The child may learn each task in such tiny fragments that the progress may go unnoticed. In this case, parents or teachers may get frustrated because they think that the child isn't learning very much when in fact they are just learning very, very slowly.

Mark continued to show very gradual progress throughout these first few years. As our family began to see what he was capable of, we began to realize that someday he might be able to do things that people didn't think were possible. Mark and I grew steadily closer as time went on. He interacted with me like a normal sibling and there were many precious moments in those years. Mark and I spent lots of time looking at books together, listening to music, playing in the wading pool that Dad got us or spending time out in the barnyard with Dad. We had a dog, Butch, at this time who was very protective of us. He would stand over top of us in our little wagon so that the cows wouldn't come near us. All in all, our family had adjusted rather nicely to Mark's disability and we were slowly learning what it took to help him.

By the time Mark was three years old, Dad had accepted his disability completely. Dad had gone through his grieving process as mentioned earlier. He had said good-bye to the dreams of Mark playing hockey or helping him on the farm. He accepted Mark for who he was and started to create new dreams for Mark. They were simple dreams such as learning how to walk or how to speak. Even though Mark was unique it never stopped Dad from treating him as a normal little boy. Dad and Mark had a very special bond. It seemed like they were always hugging, laughing or planning something to make someone else laugh. They would play little tricks on the rest of us. More likely Dad would play the trick and Mark would laugh. Mark was like his accomplice. Dad took Mark out to feed the cows or ride around in the tractor every chance he could. He would put Mark into the sled or wagon and out they'd go to feed the cows. Mark loved to ride in the tractor with Dad, probably because Dad always had music playing! (They shared the passion of listening to music.) Dad had a little red stool that Mark would sit on while riding the tractor. Mom had to help Dad get Mark into the tractor once he was older because of his size, but it never stopped Dad from wanting to take Mark with him. Dad was the type of Dad who always got down on his hands and knees and played with us. He would stop anything he was doing just to spend time with us. When we were little, he enjoyed afternoon naps on the couch with us cuddled over his stomach. Those are probably some of his favourite memories.

According to Dad, Sundays were days for family. He didn't believe in working on Sundays. We went to church most Sundays. We'd have pancakes, bacon and eggs for lunch. Dad would then take the whole family for drives in his half-ton truck and always the music from his past helped us enjoy the ride. We'd then come home for a chicken or roast beef dinner for supper. Then at 7:00 we'd all watch Walt Disney. Dad would always turn into a kid when we watched Walt Disney. He enjoyed it every bit as much as we did.

At the age of 22 months or roughly 90 weeks old, a specialist assessed Mark. At that point in time Mark was doing things at a 28- to 32-week level. Compared with children his chronological age, Mark was significantly behind and had a lot of catching up to do. At the time, the doctor felt that maybe some more testing should be done to see if someone could figure out the reason why Mark was born this way. This was important if Mom and Dad were considering having another child. When faced with the decision to do genetic counselling, my parents felt they didn't need to know the reason. To them it was just something that happened. They didn't consider the future. However, as siblings start their own families, they start to wonder if their children will be born with a disability. When my husband and I were discussing having children, it was always in the back of our minds. Was Mark's disability genetic? Would our children have a disability as well? It was only natural for us to have these questions. After many discussions, we finally decided against having genetic counselling and just decided to have a baby. We knew we'd love the baby just as much as we loved Mark.

CHAPTER 4

Mothers are amazing people, but I don't think we truly see who they are until we are mothers ourselves. My mom sacrificed more than most, and yet, to her it wasn't really a sacrifice. I'm not sure I could have handled all that she did. She has an inner strength that I can only imagine. I know she had bad days, but she always managed to handle everything God gave her. He must have known what He was doing when giving us our mother. He saw inside of her something truly special that most don't ever have.

Good mothers appear to want to do anything for their children's well-being. Our mom took that a step further. She did more than humanly possible on an average day. Instead of a career, she chose to be a mother. She brought home a son that most thought would be better in an institution. She also brought someone else's child into our home and raised him as her own, always understanding that someday he would need to meet the ones who brought him into this world. She believed in each of her children and helped guide them to achieve their goals. She wiped the tears and picked up the pieces when life dealt us disappointments. She held her son's hand many nights in the hospital and listened to doctor after doctor give her bad news. Through it all she created a home where thoughts and feelings could always be shared, unconditional love was always felt, and dreams were supported. She gave her heart and soul to her children. We haven't thanked her enough for the amazing things she has done, but there are no words that would be sufficient.

It was in January of 1980 that a very important step in Mark's future developed. Beginnings Preschool Inc. was established in Brandon, Manitoba by parents of children with disabilities. The president of Beginnings informed my parents of this program and Mark was enrolled shortly after it started. Beginnings Preschool was an incorporated non-profit organization that was run by a Board of Directors who were all primarily parents of the children involved. The Manitoba government, relevant agencies, parent fees, and community donations were used to finance this project. The program served children who lived in the Brandon and Westman area. It was licensed for fifteen children per half day. The ages of the students ranged from 3 1/2 to 5 years for non-disabled children and 2 to 6 years of age for children with disabilities. The school ran for the same amount of time as a regular preschool and was operated by two qualified teachers, parents, and of course, many volunteers. In September of 1980, the program moved to a classroom in the J.R. Reid School that was donated by the Brandon School Division. Mom drove Mark to Brandon, about 77 km, every Thursday morning for two years to help him in his development. Many days, Mom would stay with Mark during the mornings and be taught things that she could do with Mark at home. On days when I was able to accompany them, which was usually when I wasn't in school myself, I gladly went along.

In this program the children received their own individualized program to meet their needs. The regular children took part in a program that focused on social, emotional, physical, and intellectual development. This probably wasn't much different from that of the children with disabilities except for the extent of the learning. I think that this program was probably a wonderful thing for regular students because growing up with someone "different" than yourself may help one learn compassion! The school's philosophy was that all children should have the same opportunity to grow and develop in a warm, caring environment at their own individual pace. It focused on providing children opportunities to develop emotionally, socially, physically and intellectually. It also provided integration of regular and special needs children that at the time was not practiced frequently. It assisted the children and their families with programming so that their developmental lags would improve. The biggest objective was to help each child reach his/her full potential by providing all sorts of experiences for every child.

The infant stimulation program and the behaviour modification program continued throughout this time as well. Mark continued to make some progress with the help of these two programs as well as the preschool, but it was slow going. By the middle of 1980 when Mark was three years old, he could roll over, sit for a certain amount of time by himself, (but he had to be put in that position), and could bear weight on his feet. He could also stand by himself as long as he was leaning with his back against a firm surface. At this time Mark had a walker that he used around the house. He couldn't walk yet, but we hoped it was only a matter of time. Mark also had a special tricycle that he used with assistance. The tricycle was basically to help Mark gain strength in his leg muscles. Mark loved it! There is actually a picture of Mark riding his tricycle with Mom behind him for assistance on one page in the Beginnings Preschool Inc. pamphlet that was used to promote the school. Mark also used a jolly jumper to help with his muscles as well as a standing frame. A standing frame is a piece of adaptive equipment that is used to position people as if they were standing. They are strapped into it and forced to stand in that position for a certain time period everyday. He also had a platform mover that he used to move around which was to teach him how to crawl, but he never did learn that. The doctors said that Mark had very weak gross motor muscles in his arms and legs that contributed to his delay in walking. Gross motor muscles are any large muscles in one's body such as the arms or legs. A physiotherapist is someone who helps a child strengthen gross motor muscles. Fine motor muscles are the small muscles in one's body such as the fingers or toes. An occupational therapist helps children with their fine motor muscles. Over his many years, Mark had both physiotherapists and occupational therapists working with him.

I read a line in one of the Community Service Worker's notes on a visit to our home that reminded me of how amazing my mother was. It stated that Mom felt that Mark was not quite ready for spoon-feeding and that maybe it should be discontinued. The worker agreed with her. One of the biggest things in special education is learning that parents do have valuable feedback and that their opinions are often more accurate than professionals. Parents are with their children longer than anyone and they are definitely worth listening to. Throughout Mark's life, my mother learned how to be a special educator. I have come to realize that some people in this field go their entire lives without ever understanding the full experience of raising a child with a disability. Mom is one of the few people that I can talk to about my career because she understands the stresses and successes that can occur. She learned early on what worked and what didn't. She knows the ins and outs better than most. It is she who taught me how to be a special education teacher. My university professors just gave me the tools of the trade. She gave me the heart to accomplish it.

In April of 1980, Mark saw the specialist at the Child Development Clinic. He felt that Mark was progressing very well. In the Yale Developmental Schedules (a test that measures a child's development), he estimated Mark to be functioning at a 44 to 48 week level. At the time Mark was 3 years old or 156 weeks. It was at this appointment that my parents mentioned something they had noticed. Mark didn't produce tears when he cried. He made crying sounds, but tears never formed. The doctor found this interesting because there are some syndromes associated with mental retardation that do have the absence of tears. One such syndrome, familial dysotonomia, which usually occurs in people of Jewish descent; or another syndrome, themoebius syndrome, were discussed, but found irrelevant to Mark's condition. The reason still remained unknown. Mark's ability to talk also had not developed. He didn't babble or coo like babies do and he certainly had not vocalised any words. He communicated through his eyes and his gestures. We knew what a certain look or a tiny cry meant, but others often had no idea.

In the fall of 1980, I began kindergarten, which meant that Mom had Mark all to herself during the days. I imagine that this probably gave her more time to herself and certainly benefited Mark's learning. Starting school for me was a scary experience as I was a very shy child. The only two people I knew in my class were my two cousins, Steven and Tara, (with whom I'm still close). Kindergarten was a time for me to discover that other families didn't have someone like Mark. It was also a time for me to learn who I was as a person and realize that my biggest task in life would be to protect my little brother.

By this time in Mark's life, he had developed a very unique personality. Anyone who knew him well absolutely loved him. He was an easy-going child who smiled almost all the time. He was so carefree that nothing seemed to hurt him. He loved his world and everything about it. He never understood that he was different so he was completely happy. I think that for him this was a blessing because he didn't have to go through life knowing that he was different. It was the rest of us who had to deal with these situations. It also benefited him because people that got to know him realized how big his heart was. This was proven many times over the years. A good friend of mine told me once that she and her friends had fights over who was going to push Mark in his wheelchair at recess time. It wasn't until I was older that I realized that there are people out there who want to help. As a child, I always seemed to remember the negative that put a damper on our lives. Most people expect to get something from what they put in. There are not many people who just do it for the sheer satisfaction of helping a fellow person, but luckily there are some. These people are truly special and I am thankful that as I get older I am meeting more and more special people. It is always those people that I surround myself with now. Many of these people are my childhood friends because they understand and remember what our family went through.

CHAPTER 5

Even though Mark was a huge handful to my parents, they still wanted another child. Unfortunately, the doctors never did figure out why Mom had a child like Mark so they couldn't say for sure if it would happen again. They decided not to risk it, so in 1979 they applied for adoption through Children's Aid in Brandon. Before their name could be put on the list, many interviews had to take place. Children's Aid asked personal and financial questions as well as many questions about Mark. A lot of the people at Children's Aid didn't think Mom could handle another child because Mark's development showed that he might be like a "baby" for many years to come. Mom and Dad did a great deal of convincing in order for everyone to believe that they could handle another child. Mom and Dad were also asked how old and what sex of a child they wanted. They wanted a boy so they could have a normal son. Not that Mark wasn't a great son to have, but they wanted one who could play sports and help on the farm. They wanted someone that could do the things a normal son did for his family. Once Mom and Dad were accepted through Children's Aid, their names were put on a list. (The wait began which in the end was only three years, but it still seemed like a very long time.)

Mark continued to attend Beginnings Preschool in Brandon, but everyone involved felt that he needed a stimulation program on a more regular basis. At that time there was a Kinsmen school across from one of the elementary schools in Virden that was designed for children with disabilities. The only problem was Mark's age. He was a lot younger than many of the students there. Mom, Dad, and our Community Service Worker looked into the situation further and soon found a teacher who operated a preschool program in the basement of the United Church for regular children, and was more than willing to have Mark in her class. Funding for Mark then had to be found, as he would need a full time assistant. My parents tried to get funding from the government, but it was slow in coming so they decided to pay half of the fees themselves and tried to find another organization to pay the rest. The Canadian Association for the Mentally Retarded (CAMR) Virden Branch came to the rescue. They provided the preschool program with the start up money for Mark to attend. The money provided a teacher training course, other resources, and the salary for the teacher assistant. In the end, the government did finally take over the expenses. In this program Mark worked on physical, social, academic, self-help, and language skills. He attended this school for two days a week as well as the one day a week in Brandon. Between the two schools, Mark continued to progress at a slow rate. One of Mark's teachers stated that his participation in the school was a great benefit not only to him, but also to the other children in the class. They were learning how to accept children who were different. She stated that she and her assistant learned more about how children learn. From these two programs, Mom noticed that Mark's awareness of others started to increase. He started to "reach out" to others. His hand co-ordination improved. He became less nervous in big crowds, which always had been a problem. It also allowed someone else to teach Mark rather than my parents and it gave Mom a much needed break. The programs provided her with time to focus on her housework and other family members.

The skills that these two programs focused on during the 1981-1982 school year, when he was four years old, involved the physical, self-help, academic, and communication domains. In the physical domain, Mark practiced skills like walking, stair exercises, throwing a ball on command, riding a tricycle, holding on to one object with each hand, holding a crayon, and drawing a line. To help with Mark's self-help needs, drinking and feeding himself, taking his shoes off, and how to put his own jacket on were just three of the skills focused on. In the social domain, skills such as looking in the mirror to understand facial expressions, responding to his name, giving items on command, and waving good-bye were worked on. In the academic domain, work focused on following an object out of his line of vision and motor imitation (imitating certain movements). In communication, Mark practiced following the commands of give, stand up, and sit down, as well as practicing the "m" sound. Mom also continued to teach Mark these skills at home. In every domain, children learn things by imitating others. Unfortunately, no matter how hard everyone worked, Mark could never imitate. It's hard to say why, but it seemed that doing exactly what others showed him to do was just too complex for him.

In April 1982, a wonderful event happened for our family. We received a call from Children's Aid saying that a baby boy had just been born and was up for adoption. On April 21, fourteen days after the little boy had been delivered; we went to the Children's Aid in Winnipeg where a nurse, from Misericordia Hospital, had brought the baby for my parents to see. Adoptive parents, once they see the child, can then decide if they wish to take that child home or wait for another child to be born. Adoptive parents also have three months to decide if they want to keep the child, and the biological parents have three months to change their minds about the adoption. Mom checked the baby over from head to toe making sure all fingers and toes were there as well as checking to see if he seemed "normal." My parents didn't want another child with a disability as they had their hands full looking after Mark. Mom and Dad decided to take the cute little bundle home. I still remember that day as if it was yesterday. I remember sitting on the floor playing with the baby while everything was being arranged. When we got back to Virden, my parents had a doctor check the baby over to see if anything seemed abnormal. The doctor gave the baby a clean bill of health. We then had a new addition to our family, Trent Matthew Leslie.

At the time my parents adopted Trent, one of the most important aspects of adoption was to let the child know as soon as possible. Many felt that it was better for the child to know right away. That way the child didn't feel his life was a lie when he discovered the truth. Trent says he remembers my parents telling him that he was adopted, but it wasn't until he found the letters from his birth mother that he really understood what it meant. Trent's birth mother sent a letter through Children's Aid for him to read when he was ready. It explained that even though she loved him she was unsure of her relationship with the father and she didn't have enough money to raise him herself so she decided to give him up for adoption. She enclosed a picture of herself and his birth father. Trent says that this letter and the pictures have helped him through a lot of confusion he experienced growing up. Sometimes he felt sad because he didn't know his real parents, but he was never angry with them because he understood why they gave him up.

In May 2003 Trent located his birth parents. Late one night he decided to check out an adoption website on the Internet. He gave the people all the information he knew about his birth parents. Within twenty minutes, a mediator phoned him to say that his biological grandparents had been looking for him. Within a month, Trent met his birth parents. Trent still considers Mom and Dad his real parents, but he is enjoying getting to know his biological parents. It has been an emotional roller coaster for everyone involved, but long-lasting relationships appear to be developing. Trent is still happy that Mom and Dad adopted him because they have given him a great life. He claims to be blessed to have a brother who is handicapped and an "abnormal sister"!

CHAPTER 6

The first year of Trent's life was hard for my parents. It was like having two babies except that one was five years older than the other. Mark and Trent progressed at a very similar rate during the first year of Trent's life, but that was quick to change. Almost everything about that first year was difficult for Mom. When one child would scream, the other one would scream even louder. This would continue until one of them relented or they fell asleep. I became a little helper for my Mom, baby-sitting one of them while she took the other one into the store, or playing with them when she was busy with her housework. I was a busy little girl as I had started piano and figure skating lessons in the fall of 1982. Mom had a lot to handle running me to my lessons, taking Mark to his preschool programs, finding extra time to spend on Mark's development and looking after a new baby. I'm sure that Mom didn't get much sleep that year, but when she did sleep she probably was asleep within seconds of her head hitting the pillow. She remembers finding it difficult to feed Trent in the middle of the night. She felt that because Trent wasn't her biological child she wasn't as prepared as a new mother normally would be. Often there isn't much advance warning when bringing an adopted child home. Parents get a phone call and a baby often within the same week. This was one reason why she found it difficult to stay awake with Trent at night, but the other reason probably was her exhaustion from the added pressures of raising Mark.

Sometime in 1982, Mark was fitted for braces on both his legs to help his walking skills. If you have ever seen the movie "Forrest Gump," the braces that Forrest had were very similar to Mark's, although Mark never ran so hard that they popped off! Everyone constantly worked helping Mark learn to walk. Mom did many exercises throughout the day. Mark would stand for a period of time against a wall. Then he would stand for another period of time by himself. He used his standing frame daily to practice the proper position he should be in when standing. He practiced walking using a lot of physical support from Mom. They tried to have Mark walk while holding onto a walker. He practiced holding onto someone's hands and he tried to walk by himself, but success was still long in coming.

When Mark was five, Mom took him to see his specialist at the Child Development Clinic for his annual developmental assessment. The doctor found that Mark was still progressing, but very slowly. He stated that developmentally Mark was showing signs of progress with a few successes at the 18 month range but nothing higher. He also explained to Mom that since Mark was five years old, something should be done to enrol him in a regular school program. He felt that Mark probably would qualify for a grant from the Department of Education that would be about $6000.00 a year. He felt that Mark was "severely to profoundly retarded," but there was no reason why he couldn't attend a regular school.

At that time some students with special needs were being sent to other schools outside of their communities. Others were sent to different schools in their communities that were designed especially for children with disabilities. In the United States, Public Law 94-142 was passed. With the passing of this law, all children were to be educated in their home school and services were to be provided for all their needs at these particular schools. Canada soon followed suit and advocated for students with disabilities to be educated in their home schools. (A home school is the school that a child would attend if they were non-disabled.)

The idea of the IEP or Individualized Education Plan came about because of this law. An IEP is a written plan developed by a team stating the student's goals and objectives that the school personnel and parents are to work on throughout that school year. The student's background information, current level of ability in all areas, specific outcomes and performance objectives, the methods, materials and strategies needed to teach specific skills, names of all members of the team, and the plan to evaluate the student's progress should all be written in the IEP. The IEP is generally for students aged 5 to 14. Before this, a child with a disability would have an IFSP or Individualized Family Service Plan. This document is similar to an IEP except that the outcomes and objectives are for the entire family rather than just the student. When a child reaches the age of 14 and until they graduate, their plan is called an Individualized Transition Plan. This plan is again similar to an IEP except the focus changes from academics to skills needed for their future life.

Even though laws were passed, it still has taken a long time for students to be educated in regular classrooms. The idea of including people with disabilities within our school system is called inclusion. It basically means that each student should receive an appropriate education in the least restrictive environment. Today there are many different ways a student can be included within a school. Most children with disabilities attend regular classes throughout elementary school. During certain classes like Math or Language Arts, the student may be pulled from the regular classroom and attend the resource room where more one-on-one attention can be found. The resource room allows students to work at their own speed on their weak areas. As students move to junior high and senior high, it becomes more difficult to provide the necessary services within the classroom, but it is possible with the proper resources, support and training of teachers. Again the possibility of a resource room allows students more time to focus on certain academic areas while also attending regular classes. For a student with more severe disabilities like my brother, special service classrooms within the home school provide opportunities for learning life skills.

When the student's team is working through the IEP, a discussion on how included the child should be in the regular classroom is a necessity. Inclusion is a very individualized decision, and what works for some may not work for others. Some students have been successfully included in all aspects of a regular program, while others have found partial inclusion in certain areas such as gym, art or music works best for them. Every child's need is different and this should be reflected in his or her school program.

Mom talked with the Community Service Worker in Virden at that time, to see what kind of schooling Mark could have. My parents never considered sending Mark to a public school because they didn't think the school would accept him. At that time all the school-age children with disabilities went to the Kinsmen School across the street from the elementary school. Mark was more severely disabled compared to many of the other students at the Kinsmen school and they knew that he needed a lot of extra attention. In the fall of 1982, plans were still not in place so Mom continued sending him to preschool. In October of that year, my parents received a letter that would make history in the Fort La Bosse School Division. The Assistant Superintendent at the time, sent a letter stating that plans were being made for Mark to attend the regular school. It was agreed by the Board of Trustees that Mark would attend Goulter Elementary School half-days every day with an assistant. At the time I attended Mary Montgomery School, which was the other elementary school in Virden. It was thought that Mark should be at Goulter School because it was all one floor where as Mary Montgomery School had lots of stairs. It's interesting to note that at that time all the Native American children attended Goulter School while Mary Montgomery School had no one considered "different." To my parents it didn't really matter which school as long as he was getting some kind of education. They would have preferred Mark and I to be at the same school, but anything was better than nothing. Rhonda Wilton, a friend of my parents, was the assistant that was hired to work with Mark. Through her tremendous efforts over the years teaching Mark, he made a lot of remarkable gains. Before Mark went to school, there was a meeting held with my parents, the Community

Service Workers, the principal of the school, the classroom teacher, and Mrs.Wilton. At the meeting, a plan was set in place for Mark describing his goals for that school year.

The plan that was set in place for Mark's first school year was a simple one. He would attend the elementary school every afternoon. Mom was responsible for driving him into school every day and the bus would bring him home after school. The main goal for that year was to teach Mark how to walk. Communication and social skills were also worked on, but the main focus was walking. The majority of Mark's afternoon was spent in a self-contained classroom with his teacher assistant. They did a variety of exercises and drills to work on Mark's standing position, balance, and walking ability. He did spend time in other classes, but this was only for music and gym time. This helped him work on his communication and social skills.

The hard work that Mark, his teacher assistant and my Mom did throughout that year paid off. A miracle happened in the spring of 1983. My two brothers were competing to see who would be the first to walk. Everyone thought Trent would win as Mark had been trying to walk for years, but we were in for a surprise. One day in May, Mark walked all by himself. He was a little unsteady, but he had finally taken those first few steps. Everyone's efforts had at last paid off and Mark was actually walking! What an amazing accomplishment considering some doctors felt it was impossible. I guess it just goes to show that you should never say never! A few days later, Trent began to walk as well. It was probably just a coincidence that it happened that way, but it was the only time that Mark beat Trent at anything. I've always wondered if Trent did understand the significance and let Mark walk first. It's probably not very likely, but maybe someone a little higher up had something to do with it.

At this point I was in grade two and I was starting to see the world for what it was. I realized that not every family had a child like Mark. I realized just how different he really was. I realized that his needs were very great compared to mine. I also realized how ignorant, in both senses of the word, people truly were. That school year is one that I will remember for the rest of my life, as it was then that I realized I could make a difference. People say that it takes more than one person's energy to change opinions. I do agree with this, but I also feel that one person can begin the process of change. I remember an argument I had with one of my close friends about changing the world's views. He had a very pessimistic attitude. We both got so angry that neither of us stopped to listen to the other. He made the point that no one person is going to be able to change everyone's minds, but I do feel that the world can be changed one person at a time. I have seen it happen throughout my young life.

    I had a rough school year that year. I used to come home from school crying almost every day because somebody teased me about having a "retard" for a brother. Children can be quite cruel. Adults can be as well, but there is something very brutal about children's honesty. At recess time and noon hour almost everyday, I remember feeling sad because somebody had made a comment about Mark. It used to make me so furious because they didn't even know what they were talking about. Most of the children had never even met my brother so they couldn't possibly understand. I did have some good friends, but they didn't know how to help. I remember one student very specifically. He used to tease me all the time about my brother. I have always taken things to heart and usually would wind up in tears over things people said. Throughout that year I constantly tried to tell stories about the things Mark had learned. I told them what a wonderful brother he was and about his accomplishments. My telling the stories, however, didn't mean the kids were listening. It was May of that year that Mark walked. I remember being so excited that I told everyone at school how wonderful it was that Mark could finally walk. I was so proud of my little brother. I knew just how hard he had worked to accomplish this goal. I made Mom bring Mark to school so that everyone could see him walk. It was so wonderful, but the best part was that gradually my classmates stopped teasing me. At the end of that school year, I realized I had the power to create changes. The family of the boy who had teased me most owned the bakery in town and on the last day of school this boy brought me a dozen doughnuts to tell me how sorry he was for everything he had done. I look back on that day fondly and most of my classmates still remember that day as clearly as I do. I guess if I never change anyone else's opinions I have at least changed the minds of my classmates. Most of them tell me they see people with disabilities as unique individuals because of my family. Hopefully, this attitude will continue with their children. From that moment on, I became very outspoken about people with disabilities. I will probably be that way for the rest of my life. My brother made me see the beauty within people.

CHAPTER 7

Mark's walking continued to get stronger, but he still needed more practice. In August 1983, Mark had an assessment done by a physiotherapist. She stated that "his standing posture is broad based with flexed knees, in valgus position internally rotated hips, increase lumbar lordosis and arms elevated and flexed." In every day language, Mark had bent knees and held his arms out stiff when he walked. He could turn directions when walking, but needed occasional assistance. Mark had to be put in the walking position, as he could not get himself from the floor or a chair to standing position. Many muscles in his body seemed to be tight. His hips, his hamstrings, his heels, and his lower back were tight which made his gait unsteady. The physiotherapist made a number of suggestions for Mom to work on. He needed to do lots of stretching and exercises that encouraged him to change position from forward and back. He needed to practice touching his toes, walking in tight places, balancing with bouncing and jumping games in water to name a few. Mark also needed to work on learning how to get around corners and over uneven terrain.

At the age of 6, Mark had still not said any words. His specialist suggested that maybe it would be beneficial for him to be exposed to some sign language to help him communicate. Unfortunately, signing was too complex for Mark. He couldn't perform the signs, as it requires a lot of fine motor skills that Mark didn't have. It also required a solid knowledge of the English language. It was still uncertain if Mark did understand the language. It appeared that he did understand some things, but the concept of using signs to recognize words was far too difficult for him.

Our family had many traditions for every major holiday. We enjoyed spending time together as a family. Birthdays were a cause to celebrate in our house. Mom would let us have a birthday party every year. We would invite friends and family members to have supper and cake with us. Mom would make us a cake or get one specially made. We would play games in the house and have lots of fun. Recollecting these birthday parties, the same faces were often there. At Mark's parties, the faces were those of our cousins, neighbours and classmates. Usually Mark only had 2 or 3 guests attend his parties, as that was all he could handle.

In the summer, Mom would take us all for swimming lessons. Mark loved to swim! All you had to do was put his life jacket on and put him in the water. Then he would splash and swim enthusiastically! When Mark and Trent were both really little, a good friend of our family, Craig Lane, who was only three years older than me, helped Mom out at the pool. He'd carry one of the boys into the pool area or sit with us when Mom was busy with the other one. Craig and his brother, Corey, were like the older brothers we never had. We were like one big family and would spend lots of time together, especially in the summer and harvest time.

We went to the fairs in Brandon and Virden every year. The fairs were always hard on Dad because it was like pushing Mark's wheelchair through an obstacle course with all the hoses from the rides everywhere. I'm sure Dad was exhausted by the end of those fun days. Mark enjoyed the ferris wheel when he was younger. Mom and Dad could easily carry him on. As he got bigger, it was too awkward to carry him. Mark's favourite ride, however, was the merry-go-round. He would have sat on that ride for hours if he were allowed. When he was little, he used to ride on the horses with either Mom or Dad holding him on. As he got bigger, he would sit on the benches instead. It didn't seem to matter where he sat. He loved it just the same. His face would light up and he would giggle the entire time.

Harvest had its own special traditions. A family favourite was riding in the combine with Dad. We could sit for hours watching the combine do its job, talking with Dad or just listening to his radio. When Mark was younger, it was fairly easy to get him into the combine. As he got older, it became more difficult getting him up the stairs and into the combine. When Mark rode on the combine, he would rest his head on the glass and watch the grain go into the feeder. He sometimes would even fall asleep in that position. Dad never knew how he could possibly sleep like that, but he seemed to. When Craig and Corey got older, they helped Dad with the farming. They would haul grain, pick bales or harrow. Whatever Dad needed, they would do. I think Dad was always a little sad that Mark could never help him like that.

At Halloween, we carved a pumpkin that we grew in our garden. Dad, Trent and I would clean and carve the pumpkin while Mark watched, and Mom cleaned up as we went along. On Halloween night, we would get dressed up and go trick or treating. We dressed up in some interesting costumes. Mom was a good seamstress so she'd make all our costumes. We dressed up as Tweety Bird, Raggedy Ann and Andy, witches, goblins, and cats to name a few. We would go to our grandparents', friends, and other relatives' houses to get our fill of candy. We always had to keep our candy away from Dad because he loved to eat it! I guess it was a good thing that Mark couldn't eat a lot of candy, as he was able to share his with Dad.

In winter, Trent played hockey and I figure skated. Mark loved spending time at the rink. He enjoyed watching Trent play hockey a lot more than watching me figure skate, at least that's what it seemed like to me. When he was watching me, he had a bored look on his face. But when watching Trent play hockey, his face had the biggest smile. It was a dream for Dad to have his sons play hockey. He didn't need them to be great stars. He just wanted them to enjoy the sport as much as he did. Trent played well into his teen years, but Mark's disability prevented him from being anything more than a fan. My parents bought special skates for Mark once. They were like shoes that had two blades on each shoe. He tried to skate with them, but his motor skills were just not strong enough.

The Christmas season is always so magical for everyone. It has always been a wonderful time for our family. Many memories and traditions were created over the years. There were many concerts, Sunday school plays, baking, shopping, and family functions. It was lots of fun going to the mall to do Christmas shopping. We would take Mark's wheelchair, as he couldn't walk long distances without getting tired. I was allowed to push him around when I got tall enough to see past the top of the chair. I enjoyed pushing him in his wheelchair. People always stared at us, but we were kind of used to it. It didn't really matter to us, because we were proud of him. Trent and I would come up with little sayings that we wished we could have said to the people like, "Would you like a picture? It lasts longer." When we were little we never had the courage to actually say anything, but it made us feel better to think about it. As we got older we did make the odd comment. I remember Trent saying something nasty to two girls one day at a fair because they were staring at Mark. I don't remember exactly what he said, but the girls stopped staring rather quickly. At Christmas time, it seemed we could forget all our problems and try to be a normal family. Reality always set in, though, because even when we were shopping we would never be a normal family. People who know us well tease us that Mark was actually the only normal person in our family!

It always bothered me when little children stared at us. It wasn't so much the children, I guess, but it was the way the parents dealt with it. They would quickly grab their children and tell them that it is not nice to stare. I always wished they would allow the children to ask questions about Mark rather than drag them away as if he was a monster. I think the message children get when parents do that is that people with disabilities are not good enough to be talked to. If parents allowed their children to ask questions to people with disabilities, it might help them understand the situation better.

We always put up two trees in our house. One artificial tree in the basement was for all the presents from the immediate family. Then we would put up a real tree in the sun porch that was meant for extended family presents. We always helped Mom decorate the trees. Mark and Dad usually would just watch and laugh at the rest of us. There were always a few special ornaments to hang on the tree downstairs. We had ornaments that were made at school as well as the ornaments with our names on them. Mark's ornament was Rudolph with a big shiny red nose, which now I realize was very appropriate. Rudolph was considered an outcast. No one wanted to play with him because he was so different. That was exactly how Mark was treated as well. Rudolph eventually became the best reindeer of all because Santa Claus believed that he could save Christmas by using his shiny nose to guide the sleigh. When the world seemed dark, it was always Mark who guided us through. I hope that every Santa Claus has a Rudolph to believe in.

Christmas Eve was probably our favourite tradition. We would hang our stockings by the fireplace in the basement and Mom would take pictures of us separately and then all together. Dad would read "The Night Before Christmas." I probably can recite the whole story without even looking at the book because I have heard it so many times, but that was always a moment I looked forward to. Trent and I understood the story, but Mark just loved being read to. We would then set out a glass of milk and sugar cookies for Santa. Mom always did lots of baking. Her sugar cookies, made from Grandma Leslie's recipe, remains a family favourite. Then we would be sent to bed so that Santa Claus could fill our stockings and put presents under the tree. It was hard sleeping on Christmas Eve with all the excitement, and usually I didn't get much sleep. My brothers were no exception. When we knew our parents were sound asleep, Trent and I would tiptoe down the stairs ever so quietly and peek in our stockings. We would see what the other got and play with the toys that were found in them. We then would take Mark's stocking to his room so he could see what toys he got. Mark couldn't walk down the stairs very well otherwise he probably would have come with us. He was always waiting patiently every Christmas Eve for us to bring his stocking to him. He knew that we wouldn't forget about him. Trent would fall asleep quickly after discovering his stocking so I'd send him to bed.

Mark would always be wide awake so I'd sing Christmas carols to him until we were both ready to fall asleep.

Christmas morning was full of ripping open presents and getting really excited about all the new toys we received. Trent and I helped Mark open his presents every year because he did not have the fine motor skills to open them himself. It was great fun for us because we got to open double the presents. Mark always had a huge grin on his face when getting his presents. He got lots of toys that made music or moved. He was also given a lot of music tapes and music videos as well as clothes. We then would spend the rest of the day visiting with our families.

We still get together with both sides of the extended family as we did when we were little. One year we would spend Christmas Eve with the Leslie side and Christmas Day with the Hayward side. The next year we would spend Christmas lunch with the Hayward side and Christmas night with the Leslie side. We have continued to flip flop between these two sides throughout the years. Now our families have grown to nearly forty people on both sides with new additions almost every year. Christmas always meant lots of presents, but more importantly, time spent with family. We would play games or go for sleigh rides on the Hayward side. When I was younger, it was more fun to go to the Hayward side because my best friend, Tara, was also my cousin. We were inseparable when we were younger and have remained close friends to this day. Grandma Hayward always made the grandchildren sit in front of the Christmas tree for a portrait. I made sure Mark sat beside me because he sometimes needed someone to help him sit properly. It's interesting looking at all those pictures now to see how we have all grown and changed. My cousins were always so good to Mark. They accepted him for who he was and always tried to include him, although it got harder as the years went on. I remember one Christmas we all went on a sleigh ride out at my aunt and uncle's farm. It was a cold night so we all bundled up tight. We sang Christmas carols and enjoyed each other's stories. It is a very fond memory.

The Leslie gatherings hold fond memories as well. Again there were more presents, more pictures, more stories and laughter, but my favourite memories are of Grandpa singing. I will never forget Grandpa Leslie's beautiful voice and his talented guitar playing!

Mark usually enjoyed himself at our family gatherings, but sometimes when we got too loud he would start to scream and cry. He thought that when people were getting loud they were fighting and he hated it when people fought. Trent and I fought a lot at home, but we weren't allowed to fight in front of Mark because he always got so upset (although, I'm afraid, that didn't always stop us!). I remember one Christmas that all the cousins were playing in our living room. We were playing some board game that involved a lot of yelling. We had Mark so upset that we had to quit the game and find something else to do.

Pictures speak a thousand words and can show every emotion. Mom constantly took pictures of every event from the first day of school to our birthdays and every day in between. At the time I didn't realize just how precious those pictures would be. Within every picture is a special memory full of love, happiness and laughter. It is hard to go through our photo albums now. I love my little brother and I always tried to make him feel like he was an important part of my life. He is the most influential person in my life, although he didn't understand that. We always seemed to be hugging and laughing in all the pictures! Mom has pictures of us playing school. A hint of my future career I'm sure. I used to pretend that Mark was my student and would make him sit in an old desk that Dad had bought me. I don't know why he didn't ever cry because I'm sure it must have been boring for him. I like to think that he enjoyed spending time with me and from the smile on his face I think he usually did. I would spend many hours reading books with him. We would go outside and I would pull him in the wagon. Dad would sometimes get out his tractor and a little sleigh that he made to pull us around in the winter time. One time we used a big cardboard box as a carriage. We put my play horse in front of it and we pretended we were going on a ride somewhere. Mark was my constant companion in all the games that I played as a child. Those pictures are now a constant reminder of our beloved childhood.

CHAPTER 8

The summer of 1985 was an eventful one full of good times and fond memories. On the day we received our report cards in June, we left Virden for a family vacation to Portland, Oregon to visit our relatives. Anyone that knows our family well knows that we are usually running late and that first day of our trip was no exception. Picking up our report cards made us late that morning. Mark's report card conversations were often long winded. Mom and Mark's teacher had a very long chat that day that almost made us miss our whole trip. Dad was a little upset, but we did manage to get on the road to Regina, Saskatchewan with a little time to spare. When we got to Regina it took us a while to find the airport. Men will never stop for directions even if you are going to miss your flight! Finally, we found the airport. Dad dropped us off at the door so we could check in while he went to find a place to park. We had a lot of luggage as we were going to be away for 2 weeks. Mom had extra packing with Trent being only three years old. He had a very special pillow that he took everywhere as a child. Mom told him that she had brought it, but she actually only brought the pillowcase for it and put it on pillows wherever we went. Trent never even suspected a thing. Mark needed special equipment like his wheelchair and one suitcase was packed full of his special diapers. Mark was still not toilet trained so he continued to wear diapers. Mom managed to get our entire luggage checked in. We didn't have a lot of time and Dad still wasn't back from parking the car so Mom and I took the boys to the washroom. We then went to find our gate to wait for the airplane. Dad was still not back, but just as we were being asked to board the airplane he turned up. Apparently, he had a lot of trouble finding the right spot to park. He ended up going around the parking lot quite a few times before someone helped him. Amazingly enough, we were finally on our way. We had been in the air heading to Vancouver, BC for about half an hour when Trent asked when we were going to get on the plane. He apparently didn't realize that he had boarded because he never saw the outside of the plane. We had a great time on the airplane. Mark even enjoyed it.

When we arrived in Vancouver, Dad's Uncle Vern met us at the airport. We spent a few days in Hope, BC with he and Aunt Lottie. Aunt Lottie is my Grandma Leslie's sister. Our favourite memory in those few days was the trip to Flintstone Park in Chilliwack, BC. Flintstone Park was really quite neat. Everything appeared to look like it would have in Fred Flintstone's era; the cars were even designed to be driven by your feet! We had pictures taken in some of the cars and we went on a little boat ride. We also watched a performance by Fred, Barney, and Dino. The entire show was mostly singing. Music seems to be one thing that all children with disabilities enjoy and Mark was no exception. He could listen to his music tapes for hours if allowed. Mark's face lit up throughout the entire show. After the show, children were invited on stage to meet the characters. Trent and I decided that we wanted to go on stage. Unfortunately, Mark couldn't come with us because the stage was filled with people. By the time Trent and I got on stage, Barney had disappeared. We felt lucky to meet Fred and Dino, but were disappointed not to meet Barney. When we went back to find Mom, Dad, Aunt Lottie, Uncle Vern, and Mark we discovered where Barney had gone. He was sitting there singing songs and playing games with Mark. He had seen Mark sitting in the crowd enjoying the show and he figured he'd come over to introduce himself. Having a sibling with special needs does have its perks! After our few days in Hope, we headed back to the airport to fly to Portland. Auntie Myrna, Jeremy, Christy, and Shannon were waiting at the airport when we arrived. We spent a week with them in the big city of Portland. It was a week full of eventful memories. We went to the ocean and collected seashells. Mark enjoyed playing in the sand, but had difficulty walking on the beach. We went to the biggest toy store I had ever seen. We went to their cabin at Mount Hood to spend a night. Unfortunately, Mark didn't enjoy that night. He cried the entire time. We thought the altitude might have bothered his ears. We were never sure what was wrong, as he couldn't tell us what hurt; it was so often a guessing game. We went to a museum that featured the Muppet characters. We watched the movie "The Goonies" and went to the site where they filmed parts of that movie. My aunt and uncle live on the waterfront of Lake Oswego. On the fourth of July, fireworks were lit off a boat in the middle of the lake. They were the most beautiful fireworks I have ever seen. Uncle Gary, Dad, Jeremy, Christy, and I drove out to a bridge on the lake to watch the fireworks while Mom, Auntie Myrna, Shannon, Trent, and Mark stayed back at the house to watch. Mark never liked fireworks because they were very loud. Uncle Gary and Auntie Myrna's dock was over 200 steps down from their house. We enjoyed running up and down those steps! As Mark's stair ability was still limited, he was unable to go down to the dock. Mom and Auntie Myrna went shopping and left the fathers to baby-sit on our last day there. All the kids had a water fight that left Trent screaming because he fell into a wading pool. Our trip finally came to an end, but we'll remember it forever.

We had only been home for roughly two weeks when Trent had a hernia attack. One Sunday morning after returning from church, Trent started screaming at the top of his lungs. There was nothing that anyone could do to stop him from crying so we gathered everyone up and took Trent to the hospital. It was unusual that it wasn't Mark we were taking to the hospital. It turned out that Trent had to go to the hospital in Brandon for emergency surgery. My parents dropped Mark and me off at Grandpa and Grandma

Hayward's and then took off to Brandon. We were having a family reunion that day at Oak Lake beach so Mark and I ended up going with Grandpa and Grandma. By the time Mom, Dad, and Trent arrived at the Brandon hospital, Trent was in a lot of pain and very moody. The nurses tried to take his vitals when he decided to kick one of them. He also threw the thermometer on the floor when one tried to take his temperature. Mom realised while Trent was in surgery that she had not sent jackets for Mark and me. Although it was a fairly nice day, it usually is cold at the lake. My Auntie Anne, Mom's sister, came to the rescue and found jackets for us. All in all the day ended okay. Trent came out of the surgery a much happier child and Mark and I had fun at the reunion with all our cousins.

At the beginning of every school year, Mom and Dad had to attend a meeting where Mark's IEP was discussed. They found these meeting frustrating because they felt no one was listening to their opinions. The meeting always included the principal, the classroom teacher, Mark's assistant, a physiotherapist, the community service worker, and many other professionals who helped Mark throughout the school year. Mom felt inferior to them because they all had more education and this made her feel like she didn't know what she was talking about. This, of course, was not true. Parents know their children better than anyone. They spend the most time with them, and even though they may not have an education degree, they should be listened to. Parents know what they want for their child and generally are realistic about what the future holds. There are some parents, however, who have not accepted their child's disability and have unrealistic expectations for their future. It is still important to listen to what they're saying and help them deal with the situation. IEP's are meant to include the parents' ideas, but I have been at many IEP meetings where this doesn't happen. As a special education teacher who runs IEP meetings, I try to be sensitive to their situation. I now understand what my parents told me all those years. I try hard to make sure that parents know exactly what is going on in the classroom. I encourage their input in their child's school career and I share our family's experiences if I feel it might help. The only way for children with disabilities to truly succeed is if everyone works as a team. Although Mark's special service team thought they were being helpful, they actually created a lot of emotional stress for my parents. Mom and Dad never felt like they were doing enough or the right thing. My parents often came home from those meetings extremely upset.

Mark had a communication log that was sent back and forth between home and school. This was a great way for my parents and Mark's teachers to communicate. Mom would send messages stating how Mark's evening was, if he slept well, what kind of a mood he was in when he left on the bus, if he'd had a bowel movement sometime during the evening, and what he had eaten in the morning. The teachers would explain how Mark's day was, what he had worked on, what he had eaten, if he'd had a nap, if he had gone to the bathroom, and many other things that pertained to Mark's life. Communication logs are excellent for students who can't tell their parents what happened during the school day. It is a way to establish a great relationship between school and home. Mark's last teacher, Marie Plaisier, told me that she never really appreciated how well Mom communicated in his log until Mark's schooling ended. She said that she always knew what kind of day to expect with Mark after reading his communication logbook.

In the 1985-1986 school year, when Mark was 8 years old, he worked on a variety of skills. In the self-help domain, Mark worked on removing his outer clothes without assistance as well as establishing a bathroom routine. Everyone tried for many years to come up with a signal for Mark to use when he needed to go the washroom. One was never found and perhaps Mark did not have the capability to accomplish this goal. The focus went from toilet training to a regular routine for Mark to use the washroom everyday.

Mark worked a great deal on strengthening his fine motor skills. He would practice extending his fingers and wrist to reach and manipulate objects so that he could eventually play on his own. He practiced extending his index finger to poke and feel rather than using the whole hand. Mark also practiced holding various writing utensils in the hopes that he might be able to scribble on his own. Mark continued to work on his gross motor skills by practicing various exercise manoeuvres. He worked on his balance. He worked on going from a standing position to sitting on the floor and then up again. He continued to practice walking skills. An obstacle course was used for him to practice walking forward, backward, and sideways. Daily stretching, alternate hand movements, and leg exercises were also used to build his strength.

In the social domain, Mark responded well to music, clapping, and children's voices. They tried to let him be a part of group activities so that he had lots of socialization with the regular students. Most of the day Mark worked by himself in his own classroom and it was only during certain classes that he became a part of the regular classroom. Usually these times were music class, gym class, reading time and special events. Occasionally, Mark would initiate a sound or action without anyone's help, but it was rare. Most of the time he sat and watched the other students.

In Mark's communication domain, progress remained minimal. They continued to work on imitating physical gestures, verbal gestures of simple throat sounds, turn taking, body awareness with mirror work, discrimination between shapes and objects, and following simple directions.

Mark's schooling was very different from that of a normal child. He didn't take Math or English classes because these classes were useless to him. He needed to learn skills that would help him function in the day-to-day world. The goal for most children with moderate or severe disabilities is to learn to function as independently as possible within the home and community setting. They need to learn skills that can provide them with a life as normal as possible. Often these skills are within the independent living domain (cooking, cleaning, shopping, money management, dressing and grooming), the vocational domain (job-related skills) and the social domain. All children's skills are different in these areas and their school programs should focus on their individual needs. We knew that Mark would never live on his own, but we wanted him to have as productive a life as possible.

CHAPTER 9

Everyone makes mistakes and Mark was no exception. Mistakes are how we sometimes learn new skills. Mark had a lot of "accidents" shortly after he started to walk. Someone had to remain by his side for the majority of the time as his balance wasn't very good. We did try to allow him independence as his skills improved. Sometimes he made out okay, but other times, disasters occurred.

Right before Christmas in 1985, we were at the annual Wallace United Church Christmas service. After the service and the visiting, the adults were trying to put everything away. It was pretty late and everyone was tired. The Christmas service was always the last one until Easter because it was a small rural church that didn't have a good heating system. At that time, the only heat came from a wood-burning stove that was in one corner of the church. All the adults were busy cleaning up. Trent was still very small so he was sitting in his stroller and the rest of the neighbourhood kids and I were playing games around the church. Everyone forgot about Mark and just left him walking around. He found the old wood stove and set his hands on it. Mark's brain never developed normally which caused all sorts of areas in his body to not work properly. His nerve impulses didn't tell him to remove his hands from the hot stove so he just left them on. Finally someone could smell something burning. Everyone came rushing into the church area to discover Mark standing over the stove. Dad grabbed Mark and took him outside to put snow on his hands, as the church had no running water. The only part of that night I remember is seeing everyone standing around the outside door of the church gathering up snow to put on his little hands. We took him to the Virden hospital immediately. He ended up having third degree burns on both his hands, but one hand was significantly worse than the other. He was screaming because it hurt so badly as one can only imagine. He had to have bandages on his hands for three or four weeks. Mom had to change the dressings every day to make sure that the burn was healing properly. Mark found the bandages very annoying and always tried to take them off. This was frustrating for the rest of us as there was nothing we could do to help him and he didn't understand why he had the bandages on. By Christmas day, Mark had huge blisters probably an inch high that covered both palms. They were black and blue all over and looked very painful.

Mark's walking skills caused another accident. We were at Grandpa and Grandma Leslie's for our annual Christmas supper. Everyone was running around getting things organized. Mark tripped over something in the living room and put out both his hands to help ease his fall. When his hands hit the floor, both blisters exploded. Mark screamed and screamed. Nothing seemed to console him after that. I felt so sorry for him because I'm sure the pain was excruciating. We ended up going home very early that night. Eventually his hands healed, but it took a long time.

A few months after Mark burned his hands, he had yet another incident with his walking. This time it was at Grandpa and Grandma Hayward's house. Grandma had an old mirror sitting in her spare bedroom. Mark was wandering around the house like he always did when he somehow walked right into the mirror and cut his one hand quite badly. He didn't need stitches, but according to our superstitious Grandma, he received seven years of bad luck. Those next seven years of his life definitely had ups and downs, but who knows if it had to do with the bad luck from the mirror.

The one thing that always made me mad about having a brother like Mark was how much attention he got and how his life seemed to rule the world. We could never plan anything because we never knew when he might get sick, when he needed to see his physiotherapist, his doctor, or his community service worker, or when we had to go to Winnipeg to get special equipment for him. It seemed never-ending. Our whole lives revolved around Mark's. Some days it didn't bother me, but on other days it was hard to deal with. It was probably easier for me because I was older than Mark. I had our parents to myself for almost two years, but when Trent came Mark needed most of the attention. Mom feels she didn't give Trent enough attention when he was younger. She feels she was giving in to him too much instead of teaching him "no" because she didn't have the time to argue with him. She had too many things to attend to with all of Mark's needs. Mom feels bad about this as she looks back, but at the time she did the best she could with the situation we were in.

Mark enjoyed going to school very much and he was beginning to have some peers in his special education classes. As Mark got older he became more aware of the events around him. He responded to his name and seemed to know the important people in his life. He was a bubbly person and was easy to get along with when in a good mood. Mark had many friends in his school. They would take him outside at recess, play ball with him, or push him around in his wheelchair. There were many young students at school who were very good to Mark and who really looked out for him. I wish we could have been in the same school together because then I could have spent more time with him.

Mark's teacher, Lesia Wilson, and his teacher assistants worked on numerous things with him at school. They continued to work on his communication by trying to get him to respond "Yes" by moving his head. They tried getting him to look at himself in the mirror when he was making vocal sounds. They worked on strengthening Mark's fine and gross motor skills. They used large puzzles, turning pages, drawing with chalk or crayons, and finger plays to help him with his fine motor skills. They worked on climbing and crawling activities, pulling himself up, and a morning exercise program to practice his gross motor activities. All of these activities, however, depended on

Mark's moods. He had great days where he was very energetic and seemed to be observant of everything going on in the classroom. On other days he didn't want to do anything and would sometimes cry the majority of the day.

Year after year Mark's progress was always hampered by his illness. He spent many days at home. In the school year 1985-1986, Mark had already missed 32 school days by March. The doctors were trying to figure out what the problem was, but as Mark didn't speak, it was difficult to know exactly what hurt. Mark was like a frail child that was always fighting some sort of illness. Whenever someone had the cold or flu, Mark always seemed to get it and it would take him longer to recuperate. The stress of Mark being sick was hard on our family. Outings were often put off or fun activities were brought to a quick end because we ended up in emergency rooms.

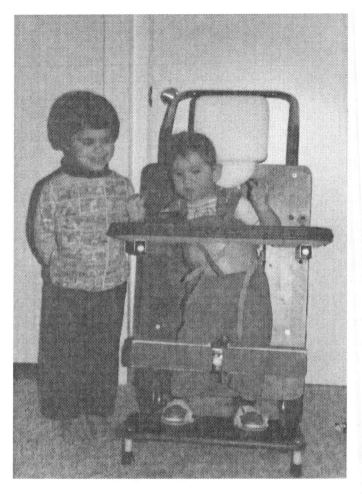

Mark in his standing frame at 19 months of age with Kim. This special equipment helped him learn to stand.

Photo Credit: Joyce Leslie

**Mark at the Virden Skating Rink at 4 years of age.
Mark enjoyed watching his brother's hockey games
and his sister's figure skating shows.
His father (Doug Leslie) is in the background.**

Photo Credit: Joyce Leslie

Mark using his walker in June 1981. This walker helped him learn how to walk even though doctors said he never would.

Photo Credit: Joyce Leslie

Kim enjoyed helping her brother.
This is a picture of her helping him
play with Play-Doh in July 1982.

Photo Credit: Joyce Leslie

Mark finally learned to walk at the age of 6.
This is some of his first steps in August 1983.

Photo Credit: Joyce Leslie

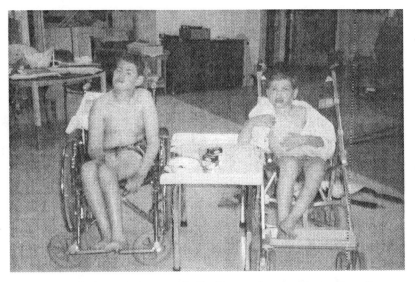

Mark and his classmate, Kelly Barnesky, before going for a swim. Swimming was a pastime Mark loved.

Photo Credit: Goulter School Staff

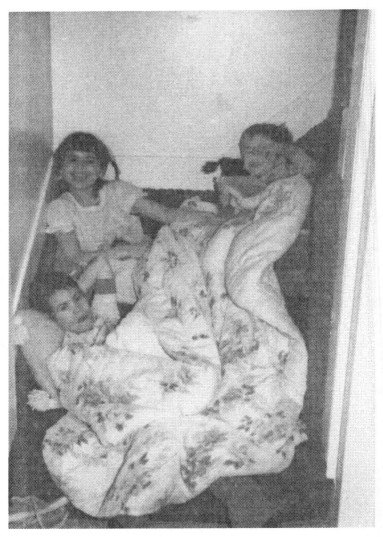

The joy of siblings! Kim, Mark and Trent
playing on the stairs at home in April 1984.

Photo Credit: Joyce Leslie

**The only time Mark saw the ocean -
our family vacation to Portland, Oregan iin 1985.
(L to R): Trent, Dad & Mark.**

Photo Credit: Joyce Leslie

Mark had some amazing teachers over the years. In the spring of 1989 Mark said goodbye to his elementary years. (L to R): Teachers' assisstants Terri Dryden, Janie Watts, Faye Rowand-Hi Eagle, Rhonda Wilton, Mark, Gwen More, Bev Eilers, and teacher Lesia Wilson.

Photo Credit: Joyce Leslie

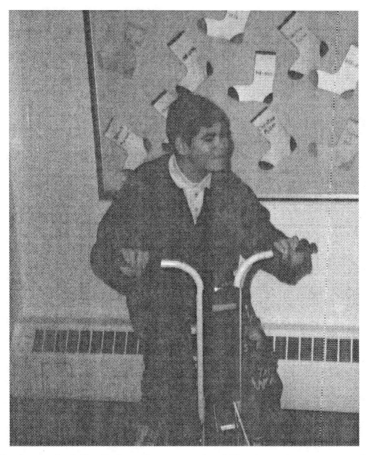

Mark needed the help of an exercise bike to get some exercise during his school days. He also had an exercise bike at home.

Photo Credit: Virden Junior High School Staff

Mark moved to Virden Junior High School where teacher, Marie Plaisier, taught him for the remainder of his school days. Here they are playing ball.

Photo Credit: Virden Junior High School Staff

Mark had to be taught to wave goodbye.
Mark is being helped by teacher assistant, Sharon Cameron.

Photo Credit: Virden Junior High School Staff

This picture is of Mark, Kim and Trent at our favorite vacation spot - Clear Lake, Manitoba in July 1991

Photo Credit: Joyce Leslie

Another picture at our favorite vacation spot in July 1992. In this picture Mark is swimming at the pool where we rent a cabin every summer.

Photo Credit: Joyce Leslie

Our last family portrait
at Kim's high school graduation in June 1993.
(L to R): Mom (Joyce Leslie), Kim, Dad (Doug Leslie),
Trent and Mark

Photo Credit: Hank Kyle

CHAPTER 10

From a June 24, 1987 article printed in the Virden Empire-Advance as submitted by Clara Miller (printed with permission from the Virden Empire-Advance):

"Mental retardation is a human condition. It is neither an illness nor a disease, nor is it "curable." It has no single cause. Causes are varied and may occur at the time of conception, through illness or accident, during pregnancy or at any time during infancy, early childhood or later life. The major causes are brain damage due to accidents, infectious diseases and environmental factors. There is a place for people with mental retardation. It is called "Society." People with mental retardation need the same things we all need: a home—though some may need extra assistance, physical help or direction, all people with handicaps should be enabled to live in their own homes. People who care for them, who will help them develop their own capabilities, provide lasting relationships and can be depended upon. A meaningful way to spend a day...at work or at school because how we spend out our day is how we define our role in society and identify who we are. Most of all the handicapped need the opportunity to learn. These people often need more intensive learning experiences and often receive less. In this area there are

many services provided to meet these needs. Pre-school classes and education in public schools, The Association for Community Living, community services workers, therapists, volunteers are just a few to mention. One such service that is just newly formed is a parent association, The Fort La Bosse Parent Support Group. Our common bond is that we all have a child diagnosed as being mentally handicapped. Our group has been formed for parents in co-operation with parents. The goals of the group are designed to meet the needs and interests of a variety of parents of mentally retarded infants, children, teens and adults. Those who work or live with mentally retarded persons such as residential staff, educators, intervention personnel and volunteers will also benefit from the group. The main goals of the group are as follows: offer support and counselling to one another, compile information of available services, increase public awareness, establish contact with similar groups in province, invite guests to monthly meetings to foster research and provide information on specific topics, keep abreast with recent developments and ensure that families are kept informed, develop educational programs for medical staff and clinicians as to the emotional and physical needs of families with handicapped children. The groups' current membership consists of parents of four pre-school children, seven school-age children and one adult. A representative of the Association for Community Living and the Community Services Worker are also members. Meetings are held on a monthly basis with the next one being planned for early September. Financial support is being received from the local Association for Community Living. It is hoped this article will reach families in the surrounding area who may wish to join the group and share difficulties and frustrations. The members of the group have faced many problems. If we can help you in any way or if you are interested in joining the group call one of the people listed."

By publishing this, it was hoped that more parents and support service personnel would join the group to increase the opportunities for the children with special needs in the community. Mom joined the Fort La Bosse Parent Group for parents of children with special needs in December of 1986. This was the first parent group in the school division. Various support groups had started in other communities and it was decided that one was needed in Virden. The reasoning behind the support group was that parents needed to play a greater part in meeting their child's needs. The support group helped parents come to terms with the child that they were raising. It also helped parents get physically involved in planning programs. It made parents feel that they were not alone in this situation. I think that every community should have this kind of support group for parents. There is a lot of pressure and stress to deal with and it is far easier if parents know they do not have to do it alone.

In the fall of 1987, the group wrote a proposal to the Manitoba Marathon Foundation to receive funding for a recreation director for both school and pre-school children. They wanted to include one-to-one integration with the children in various clubs around the community. Through the funding, each child with a disability was able to be involved in one or more activities. At that time, Mark was involved in the pioneer club in the winter and swimming in the summer. The pioneer club was for children aged 9-14. Activities included crafts, singing, sports, and bible study. Special Olympics programs were also started through this support group.

At that time, I was a figure skating coach with the Virden Figure Skating Club. I coached CanSkate at that time which involved the younger children. I remember teaching two girls with mental disabilities. Over the years, I taught these girls in skating and swimming as well as volunteering in their classroom many times. The girls were close to my age, and although I taught them certain skills, I considered them friends. I often saw them at Mark's school functions because they were in the same classes. They always stopped to chat and I was delighted to hear their stories. I regret that I don't see them now, but I remember those times fondly.

The Parent Group involved guest speakers who lectured on various topics associated with people with mental challenges. In January of 1988, the Fort La Bosse Parent Support Group sponsored a seminar by a lawyer from Winnipeg. He informed the group of the seriousness of having wills drawn up to protect the child with disabilities in case something was to happen to the parents. It was explained that at that time money left to a person with a disability would be used for residential services like an institution rather than providing them with a home in their home communities. When a parent has a child with a disability, particularly one where they would not be able to look after themselves, it is important to include a discretionary trust in the wills. The parents appoint a trustee, usually a sibling or other family member, to be in charge of the inheritance that a person with a disability would receive. The trustee would then make sure that the money is used for provisions that the person with a disability may need. The parents can state how the money is to be used as well as how the money is to be used if the person with a disability dies. Mom and Dad had a will drawn up shortly after the meeting to make provisions for Mark if something was to happen. The implications for not having a discretionary trust in a parent's will would be different today than in the 1970's. If a discretionary trust is not set up, the money a person inherits may exceed the amount that a person with a disability can have in their bank accounts to benefit from social assistance or any other benefit the government has in place for the disabled. Extra attention to detail is a must when creating a will involving people with special needs. If something were to happen to their guardians, there would have to be people willing to take on the responsibility of the child including their financial situation. Hopefully all parents of children with disabilities are aware of this issue.

In some communities (more in the United States) there are also Sibling Support Groups. Trent and I would have benefited from this kind of support, but as they are a new concept they were not around when we were growing up. Everyone often takes the time to consider the child with the disability and the parents, but often efforts are not made to understand and help the feelings of the siblings. Siblings go through a lot of emotional stress as well as difficulty understanding the situation their family is in. There are a lot of emotions such as anger or helplessness that siblings go through and often deal with themselves. There were a lot of issues I dealt with myself because I never wanted to bother my parents. Sometimes I felt totally alone in what I was feeling. I felt a lot of guilt when I was younger. I thought Mark's problem was my fault. I felt guilty for taking Mom's time away from Mark. I felt guilty when I was mad at Mark for taking attention away from me. I was mad whenever we had to change our plans because he got sick. There just seemed to be no end to the number of different emotions I had throughout a day. It seemed that no one understood where I was coming from. Trent was not old enough to understand and his emotions seemed to be entirely different from mine. Besides Trent, I sometimes felt like I was the only one with a brother like Mark. As I got older, I began to understand that I wasn't alone, but it was hard to find people who were going through the same thing.

Being the oldest child, I did what most research says I would. Most older siblings feel that they take on a parental role. In a lot of ways I was like a second mother to Mark. The research (Singers & Powers, 1993) says that the majority of older sisters tend to go into a field related to special education and that's exactly what I did. On the other hand, Trent's life took a different direction. He helps people as well by building houses and has worked at that for a few years.

The 1986-1987 school year offered many changes in Mark's programming. Mark was becoming more aware of the school routines as well as trying to initiate some vocalization or physical gestures when with his peers. Mark had a very intensive physiotherapy program designed to improve his strength and pelvic mobility as well as an occupational therapy program for his fine motor skills. Mark received extensive hand-over-hand assistance with dressing himself. Hand-over-hand is one of the techniques used to teach children with severe disabilities. When the child is learning the activity, a teacher or teacher assistant does the activity with him/her by placing their hands directly over the student's and completing the activity. As time goes on, the student becomes better at the particular skill and the technique changes to different kinds of assistance or prompts. Mark was being taught to eat independently which was something that he never could completely do. Mark was also integrated for various activities with the regular children. Some of the activities included gym classes and workshop, holiday activities, art programs, reading time and music time.

That year Mark's intensive toilet training program started. The Individual Planning Coordinator with ACL (Association for Community Living) helped initiate a program called the Azerin-Fox method. The program consisted of excessive intake of salty foods and liquids to increase the need to void and consequently help develop Mark's awareness of the process. In order for the program to work, Mark required extensive one-on-one supervision from roughly 8:00 AM to 8:00 PM to monitor the process of Mark's voiding. The program had to remain very consistent between all special services providers and the parents. The length of the program was a minimum of 3 weeks (7 days a week) with the maximum length to depend on Mark's ability to comprehend the process. A team meeting once a week was necessary to evaluate the on-going process. The program started in January 1987. Part of the routine was urinating in the toilet, reinforcement given of some kind, verbal instruction in the signalling that Mark would need to use when he needed to go to the washroom, and more reinforcement. The program didn't last very long as Mark didn't have the mental ability to understand the process.

That summer a new tradition started for our family. We rented a cabin at Clear Lake for four days. Ever since that year we have spent a week at our favourite vacation spot. Clear Lake is extremely special in our hearts. We have many great memories there and continue to make more every year. It is the only place that I feel completely at peace and the one place I can truly feel Mark's presence.

The first night of our vacation was difficult for Mark. He never was a good sleeper, but when in a new place he generally didn't sleep at all. If Mark didn't get any sleep, neither did our parents. One year Mark screamed from the moment we got there until the next day. It wasn't until the next day when we took him to the pool that we realized all he wanted was to go swimming. The cabins had an outdoor pool for all the renters to use. When we checked in at the office, Mark could see the pool and shortly after that began his screaming. Every year after that we made sure to take Mark swimming as soon as we got there. Mark definitely loved swimming. If you didn't plan on taking him swimming, you didn't mention the words pool or swimming!

In the summer of 1992, I worked as a lifeguard at the Virden Swimming Pool. That meant that, unfortunately, I couldn't go on our annual vacation to Clear Lake. Dad had also come home for a couple days to check on the farm. That meant that Mom was there by herself with the boys. I've always felt that Trent runs on solar power. When the sun gets up, so does Trent. He usually keeps going at an amazing speed all day long until late at night. He seldom sits still. In fact, I have rarely seen him sit to watch an entire movie. One day Trent, who was twelve years old at the time, decided that he was going to go fishing down at the beach even though it was cold and rainy. Trent spent the whole day at the lake fishing, but Mom couldn't stay with him. She felt that Mark would probably get sick sitting out in that kind of weather. Mom packed Mark up in the car every two hours and drove down to the lake to check on Trent. Then she would drive back to the cabin with Mark. She was worried sick the entire time that Trent would fall into the lake and drown. Trent was a very good swimmer, but you just never know. Mom didn't really know what else to do. Trent was a very independent child and he never really wanted to be "mothered" so he thought nothing of it. Mom was happy to see the end of that day and Trent managed to come home with a little fish.

Every year we go on the cruise boat. This was one of Mark's favourite activities. You always needed to watch the weather when you went on the boat because although it was nice and calm on the shore, the middle of the lake could get pretty wavy. One summer, in particular, we ended up soaking wet after our boat ride. I'm not sure that Mark enjoyed that ride! Dad would take Mark and I on the water bikes. Sometimes he would take just Mark, and that's when he got his exercise. Mark could pedal, but wouldn't pedal hard enough to get anywhere. Dad ended up doing the majority of the pedaling. We went for ice cream every day at the ice cream parlour. Mark's favourite was bubble gum, at least we think it was. He usually was very excited when he ate that kind. We went for long walks around the lake. Mark always went in his wheelchair, so Trent and I got to push him. It was very hard to take Mark on the beach, as there was no boardwalk then. Dad had to do all the pushing then because Trent and I weren't strong enough. We were always sad to leave Clear Lake. It was as if all our problems vanished when we were there. We could just be a normal family.

Mark was sick frequently throughout that year (1987). Quite often he got overtired and then seemed to get the flu. In September of 1987, Mark's doctor told my parents that Mark's swallowing muscles didn't relax. This caused him to vomit and when he got tired it became more frequent. He had a tendency to get dehydrated almost every time he got sick. Our parents had to make sure he still was getting liquids and solids into his system. That year Mark was hospitalized at Brandon General Hospital in February and then in Virden in May. We would soon learn that hospitals were to become a common place for our family. Doctors and nurses would become friends and hospitals would feel like our second home.

CHAPTER 11

The 1987-1988 school year was not a good one for Mark and it was definitely a stressful one for our family. I was in grade seven at the time and Trent had started kindergarten, so Mom finally had time to herself during the school days. Over the years, Mark had been hospitalized frequently for dehydration when he became ill. My parents felt that there was something more seriously wrong so they went to several different specialists trying to find the problem. That year Mark's health deteriorated drastically. By Christmas time, he was barely even attending school. After Christmas holidays, Mark didn't return to school because of his illness. He was in and out of hospitals and had become very weak. For four months he lived on dry cereal. He couldn't keep anything else down. It was a common occurrence for Mark to throw up at the dinner table. Our family got accustomed to that and we could eat through anything. Mom would clean up Mark and the rest of us would just carry on with the rest of our meal. In our van, we carried an ice cream pail and paper towels specifically for that purpose. Mom and Dad continued to see specialists as their concern became greater. By April of 1988 Mark was extremely skinny and very unhealthy. Finally, the doctors discovered that Mark had a hiatus hernia. A hiatus hernia is a protrusion of any structure through the esophageal hiatus of the diaphragm. Basically, Mark had an ulcer in his stomach that was causing him to throw up when he was eating. It affected his esophagus and his stomach. It was necessary for Mark's health to have surgery to tie the hernia down.

On May 2, Mom, Dad, and Mark headed to Winnipeg. Mark was to undergo surgery at the Children's Hospital at Winnipeg's Health Sciences Centre. I stayed at my Auntie Dianne and Uncle Terry's with my cousins, Tara, Darcy and Darla. Trent stayed with Grandpa and Grandma Leslie. It was a very trying time for our whole family and being separated through a very scary situation added to the tension. Everyone's emotions were constantly on edge. Trent was only six at the time so he probably didn't understand the severity of the situation. I'm not sure I did either. A person's survival depends on nutrients and Mark was just not getting enough food for his body to survive. Mark's ability to survive was starting to become questionable.

My parents stayed at the Ronald McDonald House in Winnipeg. The Ronald McDonald House is a place where families of seriously ill children can stay while the child is undergoing treatment at a nearby hospital. There are thirteen houses established in major centres across Canada-Halifax, Quebec, Montreal, Ottawa, London, Toronto, Hamilton, Winnipeg, Saskatoon, Calgary, Edmonton, and Vancouver. Each house is operated and owned by a non-profit organization led by a Board of Directors made up of business, medical and community leaders, parents, and representatives of McDonald's Restaurants. Each house runs its own fundraising campaigns. My Mom stayed at the house for the entire 3 weeks of Mark's hospital stay in Winnipeg. Dad stayed with Mom during the first few days to be there when Mark had his surgery on May 4. Grandma Hayward and Linda Lane both took turns staying with Mom during the rest of the time. On weekends, Dad, Trent and I would stay at the Ronald McDonald House with Mom.

I will never forget the day of Mark's surgery. I was worried about him and I felt like I needed to cling to something. As a child of twelve, I didn't fully understand everything that was going on, but I knew more than what everyone thought I did. My best friend at that time, who had been my friend for years, decided that she was not going to speak to me that week. I never did figure out her reason. Girls can be quite mean to each other at that age. Someone was always mad at someone else for silly reasons, like boyfriends, stealing friends away from other friends, or who was cool and who was not. It was only a few girls in our grade, but they managed to create problems everyday. I think all girls go through things like that. My best friend was usually the one to cause problems. I'm not sure why I was even friends with her, but we'd been friends for so long that it was just hard to stop. By recess the morning of the surgery, it was pouring rain so our classes were made to stay inside. I went over to ask someone on my bus if Trent had been picked up that morning. I guess I wanted to make sure he was okay. The boy was sitting with a group of friends. He must have thought it was funny. They were all laughing and being very rude. I never did get a straight answer from any of them. This upset me dearly. I ended up crying the rest of the recess. My best friend was mad at me, no one would tell me if Trent was on the bus, and Mark was having surgery. I didn't know if he was going to live or die. One friend put her arms around me and tried to comfort me. That was all I needed.

Mark ended up coming out of the surgery fine, but complications were right on its heels. He continued to throw up food when they tried to feed him normally despite the operation. He had a tube inserted into his stomach that was used to feed him for a couple of weeks.

The first weekend that Mark was in the hospital, Dad took Trent and I into Winnipeg to stay with Mom. That trip we got stopped by the police because Dad was driving too fast. Trent was fascinated with the police officer and asked a million questions before the officer could give Dad his ticket. Dad then decided that he knew a short cut to the hospital. Unfortunately, the short cut ended up being longer because we hit a few one-way streets. We ended up going down a few one-way streets the wrong way! We finally arrived at our destination. We spent the weekend visiting Mark in the hospital and at the Ronald McDonald House.

The atmosphere of the house was very loving. There were many families staying there that had children who were sick. Mom said it was comforting. She would come back to the house and everyone would talk about how their children's day was and offer support to each other. The house itself was amazing. There were many bedrooms and bathrooms in the house. Our family had two bedrooms and a bathroom to ourselves. On the main floor of the house was an enormous library. I love books so this room captivated me. There were sitting rooms on each floor that had a TV and Atari games. In the basement, there was another large sitting room with a TV, a piano (huge bonus for me as I was preparing for a piano exam the following month), and a kitchen area. The kitchen had a couple of ovens, refrigerators, dishwashers, and a pantry full of food. The guests were encouraged to buy their own food, but food was provided if the parents had a bad day at the hospital or didn't have time to go grocery shopping. There were also various toys and games in the basement and lots of comfortable chairs everywhere. The house was within walking distance to the hospital so Mom walked every day to visit Mark. It was great to spend time with Mark and our family. Being together made everything seem okay.

I sometimes wonder what Mark was thinking during his sickness. He didn't have the mental ability to understand the situation, but I'm sure he must have been scared having all those people poking and prodding him at the hospital. He would cry a lot because it hurt, but he still managed to smile.

The second weekend Grandpa and Grandma Hayward brought Trent and I in to visit. We went to the hospital, but we couldn't figure out how to get into the parking lot. We kept driving right past where we were supposed to turn. We went around and around. Dad was standing at the corridor by the hospital watching us go around and around, waving each time as we passed. Finally, we figured it out and got parked. That weekend Auntie Maxine, Uncle Barry and cousins Todd and Stacey came in to visit Mark. Stacey and I got lost in the hospital that weekend. We went to get a toy out of Mark's room for him and then we couldn't remember how to get back to the sitting room. We finally asked for directions and found our way back, but it was a little frightening.

The gastrologist, a specialist in stomach diseases, decided that maybe Mark's esophagus (throat) should be dilated or stretched. He felt that might be causing Mark's problems. Most people can have their esophagus dilated without going under anaesthesia, although, after having the process explained to me I don't think I would want to be awake. The doctors stick a huge tube down the throat to make it increase in size. It is very wide and very long. The doctors felt that it would be best if Mark was put under for this type of procedure. Once it was done, Mark's health seemed to improve. After three weeks in the Winnipeg hospital, Mark finally was able to come home.

Unfortunately, Mark wasn't home long. He was only home for two days and one night when he started to scream at the top of his lungs. On the Sunday morning of May long weekend, my parents took Mark to the emergency room at Virden hospital. The doctor on call said he'd be there in a couple of hours. My parents decided that Mark might not have a couple of hours so they drove him into Brandon. They made a good decision that day. If they had waited, it might have been too late. When they got to Brandon, the doctor was waiting. He felt that something was seriously wrong so they did a number of tests throughout the day and had him on antibiotics right away. That night the doctor shared the results of the tests with Mom at the hospital. Mark had severe infections from the gastrostomy tube. The acid from inside him was actually penetrating through his skin and burning it where they opened him up for his previous surgery. They needed to do emergency surgery on Mark right away. Mom gave her permission for the surgery, but Dad had gone home to work in the fields. They got a hold of Dad over the CB radio in his tractor and he gave his permission for the surgery. The doctor urged Dad to come to the hospital immediately as it wasn't looking good for Mark.

I was outside that night looking through my telescope when Dad came home. Dad rushed around packing clothes for us because we didn't know how long our stay in Brandon would be. That night I realized just how precious life is. Just because you always hope and pray for the best doesn't mean that is what is going to happen. I could tell by the way Dad was hurrying that something major was happening and he was scared. I have always had a strong faith in God so as soon as we got into the van to drive to Brandon I started praying. About half way to Brandon, God gave me a sign that Mark would be okay. At the time I didn't register the sign, but now I see clearly that it was meant to comfort me. I loved the stars and thought I wanted to become an astronaut at that time. It was very fitting that the sign God gave me was in the sky. A shooting star ready to be wished upon. He knew I would be watching! Now I always look for shooting stars when I need a sign. Interestingly enough, I generally receive them when I need them the most!

    Dad dropped Trent and me off at a hotel in Brandon while he went to the hospital. It was close to midnight by then. Trent and I were both scared for our brother and hungry. Neither of us could sleep so we went on a hunt for food. Dad had left us some money to use in the vending machines so we went looking for them. Apparently not all hotels have vending machines, which I did not know until that night. We looked all over the hotel and couldn't find any so I phoned down to the front desk to see if they could tell us where one was located. The lady at the front desk said that there was no vending machine. There was a 7-11 only a block from the hotel if we wanted to go there. I was very upset because of Mark so I was rather rude to her. I told her that I didn't think my brother, who was 6, and I, who was 13, should go out into the streets to find some food in the middle of the night. She probably was wondering what kind of parents left two young children to fend for themselves in the middle of the night, but I didn't care what she thought. We ended up going back to our room and Trent fell asleep fairly quickly. I sat up and wrote some nice comments on the hotel questionnaire about possibly getting some vending machines for their hotel. I flipped through the channels on TV and I was almost asleep when Mom and Dad finally got back around 3 a.m. They had brought McDonald's food for us. They must have either been hungry themselves or knew that we were starving! They were both smiling so I knew that everything had gone okay.

Mark stayed in the Brandon hospital for five weeks after that. The nurses knew our family well. We never had to report to the front desk. They became accustomed to seeing us frequently. Mom drove into Brandon every day and sometimes twice a day to see Mark. She did a lot of driving, but I'm sure Mark was glad to see her.

Mark finally left the hospital a week before we went to Clear Lake that summer. For the next two years, Mark had to have his esophagus dilated about once every year. Mom learned to recognize the signs that his esophagus needed to be dilated again. The best sign was his throwing up constantly. Mark was on blended food for about two years. Blended food seemed to be easier for him to swallow. Every time we would eat, Mom pulled out the blender and put Mark's supper in it. Blended food does not always look appetizing, especially green peas! What a way to have to eat your food! It was pretty much like feeding a baby, but for Mark at that time, it meant survival.

The night of Mark's surgery made me realize how important family is. I'm not sure I appreciated how wonderful my family truly was before this. I began to appreciate each one of them a little more every day.

The Sign From God

As our car sped down the highway on that clear dark night,
the silence was deafening.
We sat each in our own worlds, thinking our own thoughts.
I stared ahead, though not really seeing,
as the oncoming traffic traveled by.
I turned my head to look out the window beside me.
I saw the stars staring at me in their dancing mode,
as millions of thoughts of you raced through my mind.
Everything we did together seemed so special,
especially those smiles, giggles, and hugs of yours.
The happy memories seemed to drift by
as the realization came into focus.
I just didn't understand why this was happening!
Not to you, little brother, for I need you here with me.
You are my world.
Please don't leave me now!
I prayed for your survival as I felt helpless just then,
but it was as if God knew,
for a streak of light flashed before my eyes.
Watching the falling star I knew.
It was a sign from God!
I know this for sure now because you are still in my world.
And now I say "Thank you God" for leaving you here with me.

Written in June 1988 as I recalled that night's events.

CHAPTER 12

We lived seven miles out of town so we had to ride the bus to school every day. Mark needed special attention and devices to ride the bus so the school division had to have a personalized transportation plan in place at the beginning of every school year. Mom, Dad, or sometimes I when I was older, had to assist him to and from the school bus each morning and afternoon. The teacher assistants were responsible for assisting Mark to and from the bus each morning and afternoon as well. In emergency situations, the bus driver had to be trained to get Mark on and off the bus quickly. Mark sat in the same seat right behind the bus driver for twelve years. Mark usually sat alone in this seat, but I sat with him on occasion. I usually sat with him on days when I knew he was sick, when he was crying, or when he needed his nose wiped. Mark wore a safety harness that had clips attached to the equipment on the bus. It was basically a seatbelt with added support. This prevented him from falling forward or from falling off the seat. He could, however, lean over quite far on days when he was tired. The bus driver also had to be sure to have a disposable bag in case Mark had an upset stomach. Riding the bus was not an enjoyable experience for me. I remember being teased quite frequently by the students on the bus. Whenever Mark sneezed or cried, I had to go help him. One time when I was in grade two or three, I had an argument with our bus driver. Mark had started to scream at the top of his lungs for some reason. I knew Mark needed me to settle him down. I started walking down the aisle when the bus driver stopped the bus and started screaming at me to sit down. I tried to explain to him that I was just coming up to calm Mark down, but he wouldn't even listen to me. I ended up going back to my seat crying and Mark was still screaming. I understood we weren't supposed to move around on the bus, but that was a little ridiculous. I could have stopped Mark from crying. I was so mad at him that I almost couldn't speak. Fortunately for us we received a new bus driver the next year and things were much better.

In September 1988 at the Virden Junior High, a grade 5-8 school, a new classroom had been set up for the older students with disabilities. When that new class was established, the teacher made sure that every student in her class had a homeroom. The students would eat lunch with us in our classroom. One special needs student was in my homeroom and although some of the students weren't overly excited about this, I was. She sat with my friends and me. She ate lunch with us almost every day. I had known her for years so we were able to have some great conversations. She was fascinated with jewellery at the time and usually that's what we'd discuss.

Mark still attended Goulter Elementary even though he was eleven years old. He had a smaller class that school year as many of the older students moved to the junior high. One change was a new student named Kelly Barnesky. He was a bit younger than Mark, but in many ways their development was very similar. They enjoyed each other's company and spent many years in school together. Kelly's Mom, Debbie Barnesky, was very active and outspoken about people with disabilities in the community. She organized a team from Virden to participate in the Labatt Lite 24 hour relays to raise money for the Association for Community Living. I joined her team for two years during my university years and we raised a lot of money. Debbie has now started an organization (KelChris Inc.) to help adults with disabilities in their residential and vocational life. Debbie showed me just how much an advocate could accomplish.

In September of 1988, another IEP meeting occurred. Mark had many individual needs so his IEP's were pretty intense. There was a facilitator at this meeting from another organization. The facilitator is the person who makes the meeting run smoothly and helps everyone see both sides of the issue. Today there is an IEP process called MAPS (McGill Action Planning System) that many schools use to make the process more meaningful to everyone involved. In a MAPS meeting people involved with the individual (parents, teachers, the student, other family members, peers, educators and outside agency personnel) are asked many questions. The questions are: who is the person, what is the student's history, what are the dreams, what are the nightmares, what are the person's strengths, gifts, and talents, and what does the person need? After everyone's knowledge and opinions are stated and compiled, a plan of action is created. In a MAPS process, everyone involved has a chance to answer all the questions. It is a long process, but one that puts everyone on equal footing.

At Mark's IEP, his illness was discussed as well as his cognitive levels and communication levels. They discussed his strengths, needs, dislikes, and physical mobility as well as his toilet training. These various aspects became his goals and objectives. The following paragraphs describe some of Mark's goals for the year.

That year they tried to get Mark to choose his own activities during play time. Mark had a picture board with pictures of different activities. He was to show his choice of activity by pointing his finger at one picture. The teachers tried many different strategies to help Mark learn this skill. They would use a lot of verbal reinforcement when he tried to make his choice. Mark never mastered this skill and still needed lots of prompting to make his choices.

They also tried to increase Mark's awareness of daily routines and gave him more time to socialize with his peers. Mark was not overly comfortable with large crowds or strangers. He tended to get upset when new people walked into the classroom or into our house. He also would get very upset if there were too many people around. Mark's teacher tried to help him overcome this by setting up situations that he would have to deal with. Examples of this include taking Mark into the hallway at recess and outside with the other students at lunch. The teachers also took Mark to all assemblies as it was often a large crowd and very noisy.

The teachers also worked on many communication goals. They worked on using pictures to communicate, using eye contact, increasing Mark's production of various sounds, and increasing his receptive language. Receptive language is defined as how we receive the message being sent to us. It was hard to know how much Mark truly understood, and because of this, he was hard to teach. Some days it seemed he understood and other days it seemed he didn't understand anything. His understanding seemed to correlate with his daily moods.

Exercises were done to strengthen his fine motor and gross motor skills. The teachers would place Mark's toys out of his reach so he had to stretch his fingers and arms to reach the toy. They did activities where they explored different textures and materials so that Mark could learn to recognize tactile differences of common objects. Mark continued working on his balance by walking on uneven surfaces or around obstacle courses. Physio exercises were done to rhythmic motions because of Mark's enjoyment of music. They used a stationary bike for leg exercises. The pedals had loops on them so that Mark's feet wouldn't slide off. Mark would get lazy and just stop, but if his feet were attached he didn't have much choice but to pedal! Mark enjoyed riding the exercise bike at school and eventually we had one at home for him as well. Mark also practiced sitting on a ball for balance development and walking up and down stairs to practice those movements.

As Mark still had not mastered feeding himself or dressing himself, these were still considered goals for him. Mark's toileting program was readdressed that year. The program had been put on hold due to Mark's sickness the previous year, but it was decided to restart the program. They began his toilet training program again in January where he was toileted regularly and out of his diapers at school. Unfortunately, the program did not progress as effectively as everyone had hoped. He was capable of doing most of the steps, but they couldn't establish a means of communicating his needs. They also had trouble getting him to stay dry consistently between bathroom visits. It seemed he just didn't understand the process.

Mom and Dad were excellent at attending all our functions as they felt it was important to be there so over the years Mark had to follow Trent's and my busy schedules. Because he couldn't communicate, he couldn't say, "No, I don't want to go" so he was taken to skating rinks, baseball diamonds, curling rinks, and swimming pools. Sometimes Mark would cry and make a fuss, which possibly meant he didn't want to be there, but usually he enjoyed watching the activities. Most weekends Trent would be going to one town participating in some sport and I would be going to a different town. Often our parents had to split up and go different directions. One time I had figure skating tests in Foxwarren, Manitoba. Mom and Trent had already left for his activity when we realized that Mark was sick. Dad threw a couple of ice cream pails, some paper towels and a change of clothes for Mark into the van and away we went. Mark had to stay at the rink all day even though he was sick. We didn't have much choice in the situation, but Mark must have had a lousy day! It's a good thing I passed my tests!

Mom remembers Trent and Mark's relationship as being somewhat stormy. There was five years difference between their ages, but their development was very much the same for the first year. In a lot of ways their relationship was more like that of normal siblings. They got along fine one minute and the next Trent was getting angry with him, biting him or taking his toys away. Trent, however, remembers the relationship differently. "It was pretty good, I think. I don't really remember a lot when we were younger." He did remember having to protect his brother, though. "I used to hate it when people stared at Mark. I would get really mad and snap at people or say things like 'would you like a picture?'"

The research says that younger siblings often find it difficult when they master skills that their special needs sibling has not yet mastered. Trent doesn't remember ever feeling this way and Mom doesn't think it even bothered him. Research (Powell & Ogle, 1985) also talks about siblings feeling pressure to make up for the child with a disability by being "extra-good." Trent says he never felt that way except he did feel that he had to be the son that helped Dad on the farm. It wasn't pressure, but a responsibility that he didn't always want. Trent's personality was probably reflective of the situation he was in.

Trent is a brother that Mark and I both loved, but I didn't always understand him. He's the brother that completely dominates conversations with his interesting stories or his sense of humour when he's in the room. He can make conversation with anyone and knows people from all over the country from all walks of life. He has the charm to make everyone laugh out loud. He can walk into a room and instantly be centre stage. I always thought that Trent could truly shine someday. As a small child, he could play right to an audience by getting "down" or singing his favourite song. I remember one Christmas concert when he was about six or seven. His class did a musical number for the concert and all I remember is Trent being smack dab in the middle pretending to play a guitar and singing as if his life depended on it. As he got older, he struggled with his identity and became more conscious of his appearance. Thus his impromptu performances ceased, even though we all wait to see them emerge again someday. He sings in the shower, when he is alone, or anytime he thinks no one will hear his voice. Someday I hope that he finds his confidence to let his talent shine.

Trent has often reminded me of Brad Pitt's character in the movie *A River Runs Through It*. He had more spunk and energy than either one of us. Trent has always lived for the moment and didn't think of the consequences of his actions. He has the courage to stand up and say, "This is who I am and if you don't like it, too bad." He won't change his personality for anyone, maybe just some of his habits. His wild streak of not conforming to rules has caused him to go through a lot of rough patches over the years. He had trouble in school and battled depression through his teenage years. He seeks out people who have had a troubled life and he often tries to help them.

Unfortunately this compassion has caused him heartache over the years with people using him for their own purposes. But no matter what is happening in his life, when he's in a good mood, he can bring everyone else to his level. He can make us all laugh so hard we're crying, but at the same time we worry for him. He wears his heart on his sleeve and has a side that is more vulnerable than any of us realize. Lots of times people do not understand those that we love best, but that love helps us through what we don't understand. Even though I never fully understood Trent and his actions, I still loved him like no other.

Trent says the experience of having a sibling with a disability was a positive one. "I got an opportunity that others didn't get. It has given me a different outlook on life than others and we are a closer family because of it." To him it doesn't matter what happens in our lives, he knows we will always get through it together.

CHAPTER 13

    Mark finally moved from Goulter Elementary School to the Virden Junior High School in the fall of 1989. Marie Plaisier, the teacher, and her assistants should be credited for a lot of Mark's acquired skills. When most children with moderate or severe disabilities reach the age of twelve or thirteen, they are placed in a life skills program. The focus is moved from academics to skills that would be needed in future residential or vocational situations. Activities should include housecleaning, cooking, shopping, money management, job-related skills, leisure activities, and social skills. The classroom at the Junior High focused on these skills, which was the reason for Mark's change in programming. Because of Mark's severe disability, many of these skills would never be learned independently, but would need constant supervision. Mark eventually acquired some steps to accomplish certain tasks, but never enough to live on his own.

    Mark's school program continued to focus on some main areas. Communication was still the most important. Mark could keep eye contact with someone and seemed to concentrate on what was being said. However, Mark had no way to communicate with others. School personnel and our family learned Mark's body language and the differences in his vocalizations. It was very similar to communicating with a baby. If you are around a baby for a certain length of time, you learn their different cries. We learned what certain looks or what certain cries meant. Mark would flash a huge smile or giggle when he was excited about something. He would cry really loudly and constantly if he was unhappy. People that weren't around Mark had a harder time communicating with him, which was why he needed a system of communication. The school tried to teach him sign language, but was unsuccessful due to his weak fine motor skills. Mark's teachers tried to teach him to use communication boards. This involved a higher level of cognitive ability than what Mark was capable of. He did use the boards somewhat, but it was so inconsistent that no one was really sure if he was communicating.

Communication boards involve picture symbols that people point at to tell someone what they want. For example there may be a picture of an apple and then another one of someone eating. If the person points to the person eating and then to the apple, it would mean that they want to eat an apple. A communication board can range from a couple of pictures to layers upon layers of pictures in a binder type format. When a teacher first starts to teach someone how to associate pictures with symbols and words, they usually use a camera to take pictures of real objects. These pictures are then used with the child so they can associate the word with the picture. As the child begins to understand, the teacher adds the symbol picture and takes away the real picture. Then they gradually move from a few symbol pictures to a wide variety of pictures. The symbols are then grouped into categories based on when and where the student might use the word. The symbols are placed on a board for the student to carry around everywhere they go. Some individuals carry their boards in a type of wallet while others carry them in a binder format. There is computer software on the market today that teachers use to create these communication boards.

With today's technology, many people with communication disabilities are using special devices to help them talk. A "Dynavox" and a "Dynamyte" are just two examples. Lots of communication boards can be programmed into these devices for a student to use.

The student can then move around on the screen until they find the page or board they want. Depending on the type of machine, the person can either type their message, use their fingers to select pictures, or use switches activated by their mouths, fingers, toes, or head to activate the computer voice. The "Dynavox" is fairly bulky and is generally used by individuals in wheelchairs as they can set it on a tray across their laps to use. The "Dynamyte" is more compact and can be easily carried around anywhere the individual needs to go. Many of these types of devices are relatively new and were not available when Mark needed them, but simpler ones were starting to come on the market. There are many computer devices on the market that can be adapted to each individual depending on his/her level of ability.

A lot of Mark's toys were converted to switches to help him learn. Mark loved sound, light and movements, so many of his toys were fixed to sing, light up or move. A switch was placed on the toy and hooked up to the device. Mark was then taught how to move the switch to see his toy in action. Most of the switches were something that Mark just had to touch with his hand to activate. Sometimes he had to move a button over to activate it. This became very useful when using the computer, VCR, or stereo. At school the computer was hooked up so that Mark could run the programs by switches. One program, for example, sang songs when Mark touched the switch. As soon as he hit the switch, the song began. On Mark's stereo, tape was put over all the buttons except the play button. This helped Mark so that he knew which button to push to make it play. Mark also learned that if he hit all the other buttons the tape would stop and eject itself. Over the next couple of years, Mark learned how to play his own tapes himself. When left in his room, he could put the tape on and flip it when it was done. This was a great skill for Mark to have acquired. Before he learned this skill one of us had to flip his tape every time it was finished. One day, Dad could hear Mark playing with his tapes and it sounded like he was having trouble with something. Mark banged around for a good ten minutes before he gave up. Finally, he walked out to the living room and handed the tape to Dad. I guess that was his way of saying, "Hey Dad, I need help!" This event showed that Mark could initiate an interaction if he really wanted to.

Mark continued to have an intensive physiotherapy program to increase his fine and gross motor skills. He had fallen arches on his feet, but shoe supports seemed to help him walk better. He also had knock-knees that turned inward, poor balance, weak quadriceps, poor arm extension and bilateral movements. The school continued doing various exercises to strengthen all of these areas. Mark used a soft ball between his knees to encourage suitable spread of his legs and use of his quadriceps. He practiced walking through obstacle courses to teach him to regain his balance. He continued to practice walking on a variety of surfaces and different levels of terrain to help his balance and stability in different environments.

Mark continued to need help with his dressing and eating skills. He had to be taught to lift his feet in and out of clothing, how to undo his shoes and remove them, and how to pull off his clothes. Mark had a certain undressing routine that he followed every morning when he reached school. After learning the basic language of "on," "off" and the clothing names, Mark worked on undressing and dressing himself. He started the routine by removing his toque and mittens during the winter. He then pulled down the zipper of his jacket, pushed the jacket back off his shoulders, and removed one hand and then the other hand. Then he had to hang his jacket on the hook in his locker. Mark then sat down on a chair, reached for his shoelaces to pull and loosen them. He pushed his boot off with his hand on the back of his heel. After he removed both shoes, he pulled the zipper down on his ski pants and then pushed his ski pants down to his knees. He then supported himself with one hand on either a table or chair and stepped out of his pants one leg at a time. These steps were then repeated in the opposite direction when Mark went home from school. The teachers always verbalized what Mark was doing with each action to help him understand and reinforce communication. Prompts and hand-over-hand assistance were only used when Mark needed encouragement to follow his routine. Mark could undress himself fairly well, but needed help tying his shoes and putting on his ski pants. It seems strange to think that a twelve-year-old boy couldn't do something as simple as dressing himself, but Mark couldn't. The skill had to be broken down into simple tiny steps so he could learn to complete the task. This skill took Mark many years to master and he often still needed some assistance.

Mark continued to work on his toileting skills. To help Mark communicate his need to go, the teachers used a signal and the word "bathroom." The teachers took Mark every half hour at the beginning of every school year. Then, once they figured out his routine, they took him approximately every hour and a half. Mark's bathroom routine was taught in the same way as his dressing routine. Mark was prompted to move towards the bathroom with a light touch to the back if movement was not initiated independently after the signal was given. After the verbal instructions from the teacher, Mark turned the light on in the bathroom and lifted the lid of the toilet. He then stood in front of the toilet and pulled down his pants and underpants/diaper. He then sat down and hopefully went to the bathroom. When Mark was done, he was prompted to stand up and flush the toilet. He pulled his pants up, washed his hands and dried them. He opened the door and turned off the light. Mark became accustomed to his bathroom routine, but assistance was always needed.

The fall of 1989 marked many changes in my life. I started high school at Virden Collegiate Institute. I had my first boyfriend that year and I started spending more time with my friends than my family. My parents had relied on me to baby-sit, but as I got older I wanted to go out myself. I spent many weekends and holidays baby-sitting Mark when I was younger, but when I was in high school I wanted to be anywhere else but home. My parents then started to depend more on respite workers. A respite worker is someone who is paid by the government to look after a child with a disability while the parents take a needed break. All parents need breaks from their children, but a child with a disability is so much more stressful on adults' lives that breaks become a necessity. My parents didn't go out that much, but as they started to find more people capable of looking after Mark they began to go out more. We had many respite workers over the years that did a great job looking after Mark. One special respite worker, Terri Dryden, deserves extra credit for all her support to Mark and our family. She was Mark's main respite worker for many years. She not only provided care giving during the summer and on weekends, but was also one of Mark's teacher assistants for many years.

Children with moderate or severe disabilities often forget some of their acquired skills over the summer months. Therefore, it is essential for them to have continual programming even in the summer. Through Child and Family Services, summer programming for these children is often used to help retain skills learned during the school year. Mark spent two afternoons a week for many summers with different respite workers. They worked on many skills from his school program. Mark's summer program gave Mom a break as well as helped Mark retain his skills.

Mark was healthier now and could eat most food normally. Mom still blended some of his foods, but it was mostly the ones Mark found difficult to swallow. He still got really sick when he did become ill and still managed to wind up in the hospital for a few days every year. The doctors knew what the problem was now so they continued to dilate his esophagus when needed.

CHAPTER 14

Mark's program in the 1990-1991 school year still addressed four main areas: physio (fine and gross motor skills), self-care and life skills, language and communication, and social and emotional growth. Skills in each area basically remained the same as in past years, but the activities that were used to teach Mark's skills were continually changed.

When working with children with disabilities, it is very important to keep in mind what type of activities their peers would be doing. This is much easier with younger children, as it is still appropriate to do "little kid" activities such as reading children's books or playing children's games. When the child gets older, it becomes more difficult to find age-appropriate activities especially when that child's mental ability is the same as a five year old. Mark probably functioned between a two to four year old level. Most of his skills were at the two year old level, but some skills were at a higher level. For this reason, it was difficult for Mark to participate in the normal activities of a thirteen year old.

Mark's long-term goal in the physio domain was to continue to develop skills that promoted full extension, a sense of balance and strength in his fine and gross motor skills. At school, Mark did a physio routine to help build his stability and strength. Using a rebounder, exercise bike, walking on stairs, walking on uneven surfaces, reaching and stacking objects, and pushing and carrying objects are just some examples. The physiotherapist did a reassessment in October 1990. She found that Mark's strength in his lower limbs had improved and even though his gait was considered slow, he had improved. Mark had a lot more stairs to contend with at the Junior High, but he managed quite well to use the stairs with two railings and assistance. The physiotherapist's recommendation was that Mark needed physical exercise to improve his balance, upper limb strength, and coordination. One of her suggestions was for Mark to practice walking on a board, tape or string line with and without shoes to improve his balance. From this assessment Mark's physio program was developed for the year, but really it wasn't any different than previous years.

At this time, Mark did not see an occupational therapist (someone who helps to strengthen the fine motor skills) on a regular basis. Therefore, Mrs. Plaisier applied for occupational services for Mark. In December of 1990, an occupational therapist did an initial assessment on Mark. She found that his hands were held with thumbs resting in adduction. This meant that his thumb always rested across the palm of his hand. He used a pinch grasp (used his thumb and forefinger) when picking up objects and his fine motor coordination was minimal. The occupational therapist had many suggestions for the school program. She felt that he needed appropriate chair heights to encourage proper sitting posture. Mark hunched over when sitting because of his curved spine. He needed to practice a variety of exercise movements such as swinging his arms, rocking back and forth and touching his toes to music. He needed to work on pouring things such as milk or juice. He needed to be encouraged to scribble with an eraser, chalk and a blackboard. She felt that an auditory component should be used in Mark's pre-writing activities such as painting with a musical toothbrush or attaching bells to his markers. Other activities that were mentioned included finger-painting in whipping cream, drawing on cake frosting, drawing with cheese spread on crackers or bread, writing on sandpaper, drawing with a finger on yarn or string shapes, drawing in sand or mud, and using finger paints, lotions, pudding, gelatin, or oatmeal to draw. Some of these activities became part of Mark's daily program to improve his fine motor skills.

Both the physiotherapist and the occupational therapist felt that Mark needed arch support and firm shoes or orthoses to assist his walking. Orthotic devices are any device used to brace a limb or spine to aid in gross or fine motor activities. An application was sent to the Manitoba Health Services Commission for Mark to receive orthotic devices. After an orthotics assessment, it was decided that Mark needed a bilateral ankle foot orthoses (AFO). This basically was just an insert molded to form his feet. One was made for each shoe to provide better ankle support.

In the classroom, Mark was encouraged to participate in independent living skills such as cooking and cleaning within a lunch program. In the special needs classroom at the Junior High, the lunch program involved the students making lunch for themselves three times a week. They learned how to shop, how to prepare the food and how to set the table. After preparing their meals, all the students ate together to practice proper meal manners. They would then each take their dishes to the sink and take turns washing the dishes over the course of the year.

Mark's toilet routine was again part of his self-care program. The driving force behind the constant need to toilet train was the expense of Mark's diapers. The diapers had to be specially ordered through the Health Unit and they cost roughly $2000 a year. Luckily, Mom and Dad were able to claim some of this cost on their income tax as a deduction. If one is mentally or physically handicapped or if your child has any other type of disability, you are eligible for certain income tax deductions. The Government of Canada has a Disability Tax Credit that parents of children with disabilities can benefit from. In order to receive this non-refundable tax credit on your income taxes, one must fill out a form to determine if the person with a disability is eligible for this special benefit. A doctor, psychologist or other specialty professional has to complete a form stating how the disability affects the person's life. If the person is blind, needs life-sustaining therapy or has difficulty with any basic activity needed for daily life (walking, speech, hearing, dressing, feeding, elimination, perceiving, thinking or remembering), they would be eligible for this benefit. The disability also needs to be severe and prolonged in order to apply. The amount that a person can claim often differs from year to year so it is important for parents to be aware of this benefit so they can fill out their income tax forms properly each year.

Other issues in the area of self-care included encouraging Mark to feed himself and make choices about what he would like to eat, dressing and undressing himself with little assistance, using a routine to properly groom himself like brushing his teeth after every meal, and working on his wheelchair skills so that he could learn to work it himself. Mark only used his wheelchair when we went shopping for the day, went to fairs, or any special activity that would involve doing a lot of walking. He didn't know how to wheel it himself so it was a skill that he needed to learn. He worked on how to fold and unfold it as well as how to move it on flat surfaces and through doorways. All of the self-care skills were taught with a lot of verbalization from the teacher and teacher assistants as well as hand-over-hand prompting to help him establish the skills in the first place. Everyday these skills were a part of Mark's school routine. He performed his bathroom routine approximately every two hours. He practiced undressing himself when he got to school and dressed himself when it was home time. He practiced his feeding skills when he ate lunch and when the class had snacks. He practiced his grooming skills after he ate lunch everyday, and he had a daily wheelchair routine.

In Mark's language and communication program, again the emphasis was on finding some way to communicate whether it be by pointing or signalling. Situations were set up during the school year where Mark had to make choices and use his communication skills to relay these choices. To improve his social and emotional growth Mark participated in music class, swimming, assemblies, and other school activities. A Circle of Friends program was also established to provide all the students in Mark's classroom time to practice their socialization skills. Regular peers came in at recess and noon hour to visit with the students. These students would either play games with them in the classroom or take them outside to interact with other regular students. There are lots of Circle of Friends programs run in many different school divisions across the province. Each program is run differently depending on the needs of each student. Sometimes the regular peers are only involved with the child with disabilities at school while other programs help the child become involved within the community. Mark's Circle of Friends program was limited to the school environment.

In April 1991, I turned sixteen and got my driver's license! My parents were very happy about this considering the many hours they spent as chauffeurs running me to figure skating, piano, coaching, baseball, and swimming. Mark was probably happy as well because it meant he didn't have to spend hours at the cold rinks, at baseball diamonds getting eaten by mosquitoes and hours at the swimming pool watching Trent and I take swimming lessons. (Mark's swimming lessons were included in his summer programs. They were usually at a different time than our lessons.) Unfortunately, I had a car accident two weeks after I got my license. Teenagers seem to think they are invincible, but they aren't. One morning I had to take Trent to school because he needed his bike in town. I was upset about this, as I had to get up earlier! I'm not much of a morning person so getting up earlier was not a good thing. I had a typical "teenager" attitude that morning and we ended up running late. I was driving very fast on the gravel road by our house when I hit loose gravel. The car started to fish tail and I slammed on the brakes, the worst thing I could have done. We ended up in the ditch upside down. It was a very traumatic experience for both Trent and me, and I certainly learned my lesson. I never go over 70 kilometres on gravel now! I'm pretty sure I wasn't allowed to drive with my brothers for a long time after that!

When a family is living through a situation like ours, the support of extended family and close friends becomes an essential lifeline.

Our extended family supported us in a variety of different ways. Most of the time that involved babysitting time, visits to the hospitals and emotional support. Every summer we spent time at both our grandparents' places. Trent and I both would spend a few days at each place with cousins at different times. This gave Mom more time to spend with Mark. Our grandparents and older cousins also babysat Mark when Mom and Dad needed a break. Grandma Leslie still has the blanket that she used to sit Mark on when he came to visit. You never knew when Mark was going to throw up so it was always a good idea to put something under him if you didn't want the carpet stained. That blanket must be pretty sentimental for Grandma to have kept all these years. As Mark got older, however, his needs increased to the point where only I or a respite worker could baby-sit.

When we were younger, we spent vacation time with aunts, uncles and cousins to help take our minds off Mark's problems. There were many weekend holidays, day trips to waterslides and trips to Oak Lake beach. During these fun times, we left our problems at home and enjoyed the relaxing times. It was fun to spend time with our cousins and these are times we remember well. Unfortunately, as Mark got older we couldn't keep up to the others during these trips so we began vacationing by ourselves. With Mark it was like travelling with a baby. You couldn't just pick up and do something spontaneously. It involved a lot of thought and planning time to do each activity.

Although our extended family was a great support system, Mom and Dad felt they didn't understand how different our life was. Mark's problems didn't really affect how our extended family lived. Their lives were still normal and most of the time they didn't realize everything that was happening in Mark's life. They tried to be as supportive as they could, but they just didn't understand the problems that we had. Because of this Mom and Dad became very independent. They often wouldn't discuss their problems or ask for help because they didn't want to impose. Instead they turned to Trent and I for the support they needed and Trent and I turned to each other for the support we needed. Because of this our immediate family became extremely close as we learned to deal with so much by ourselves.

Mom and Dad feel they lost some friends when Mark's disability was discovered. They have many theories on why this happened, but no real proof of the reason. One reason may have been that their friends just didn't know how to handle the situation. Another could have been because we couldn't do the same activities as other families could so we got left behind. It also could have been because my parents began to put all their energy into their own family. They realized that their three children needed special support because of Mark's disability so they pushed themselves away from certain friends.

Even though they feel they lost some friends, the ones that stayed have kept us afloat over the years. Our biggest support probably came from the Lane family. Bob and Linda have been the ears that listened when Mom and Dad needed to talk. Craig and Corey helped Trent and I have fun by doing "normal sibling" activities. They kept us laughing and are an important part of our family. We know we can call them any time we need them. Unfortunately, Corey passed away in 1998, but he still watches us from heaven.

Trent and I both have a great circle of friends who have been there when the going gets tough. They provided us with shoulders to cry on, outlets for our anger and helped to keep us smiling. Most of my close friends have known me since elementary, junior high or high school. Lorry Hall and Marcie Dunn are two friends who have been there for me since elementary school and Erin Brown, Brenda Stewart, Terri Rookes, and Krista Stowe have been there for me since high school. Those six know everything! Over the years I have realized that old friends can never be replaced. They have watched you grow up. They have been there through all the tough times and all the happy times. My old friends know every story because they were there. They know exactly what a certain look on my face means and they know exactly how to respond. Sometimes I think they know me better than I know myself. My new friends have listened to my stories of Mark and have been supportive of my career and interest I have in helping people with disabilities, but because they never met Mark it's hard for them to truly understand.

Mark's circle of friends consisted of his classmates at school. They enjoyed their school days together, but never spent any time together outside of school. This is often common for children with disabilities. Mark spent all his time with his family, and he enjoyed every minute. When people with disabilities become adults, their circle of friends often remains as those classmates that they went to school with. They often are the people that the person with a disability lives with or works with and they usually have the most in common so it becomes a natural friendship.

Despite the ups and downs throughout our life our circle of friends and our extended family have grown over the years and we are glad to have each one of them in our lives. Each person gave us something different that we needed. There really are no words that can truly describe the support we have received from our friends and family. There will always be a special place in our hearts for each one of them.

CHAPTER 15

As Mark, Trent and I grew up our life focus began to change. In October of 1991, I got my first job at the Chinese restaurant in Virden and had a new boyfriend. My job, my boyfriend and going out with my friends meant I was seldom home. I saw less and less of Mark, but I did try to spend as much time with him as I could. Usually the time I spent with him was late at night when everyone else was sleeping. Mark didn't sleep very well and was generally awake in the middle of the night for a couple of hours. When Mark was younger, he would cry to get my parents up with him. As he got older, he found things to amuse himself in the middle of the night like his music and toys that he slept with such as his A&W Bear and his Bugs Bunny. Usually, Mark would fall back asleep on his own so Mom and Dad only got up with him when he cried. He generally only cried when he was thirsty or needed his diaper changed. On weekends, I would come home late after working or being with my friends and would check to see if Mark was sleeping. He was usually up and it seemed as if he was waiting for me. These special times strengthened our bond. I would tell him what I had done that night. I would talk about my feelings towards my friends, boyfriend, or myself. Mark was truly my best friend in that I could tell him anything and know that he wouldn't tell anyone. I trusted him with all my heart. Mark was the kind of friend that every teenager needs. He would listen to me for hours if I wanted him too. He never judged me and he couldn't give me advice. All he could do was listen and that's what every teenager needs. He allowed me to sort through my feelings just by letting me talk about them. Most things he probably didn't understand, but he understood my tears and my laughter. When I cried, he gave me one of his monster tightening hugs. When I laughed, he would laugh with me. We had a bond that no one can ever replace. In a way we were soul mates because we understood without a word how the other was feeling. Most brothers and sisters don't have that kind of relationship, and I feel fortunate that we did.

In September of 1991, Bill 47 became part of Manitoba's Highway Traffic Act. Bill 47 stated that it was illegal to park in reserved handicapped parking unless the vehicle had a permit. This developed into the Parking Permit Program. There was a program prior to this, but it wasn't efficient. For instance, we would go to various places like shopping malls or hockey rinks and have to park so far away that Mark could never have walked. Someone was always parked in the handicapped spots that shouldn't have been. Dad ended up dropping Mom and Mark off at the building's front door and then parking our vehicle. We received our updated parking pass in November 1991. With the passage of Bill 47, as well as the $100 fine for illegal parking, the new permit was more efficient. Occasionally, however, we did encounter problems. Sometimes we would find that people without permits had parked in the reserved spots. Other times people with the permit would park there even if they didn't have the person with them that the permit was needed for. We were never allowed to use our permit unless Mark was with us. Dad said that someone else needed it more than us. It always bugged me when people parked in those spots without a permit. People should have more respect for those that do not have the capability to walk great distances. People should be grateful that they can walk long distances and enjoy that simple pleasure that some can't!

Nowadays, people are trying to make their towns and cities more accessible for people with disabilities. In fact, it is law that all public businesses are wheelchair accessible. This means ramps, handicapped washrooms, and accessible doors must all be built into buildings. It's also important for the average person to be more aware of these things. People can be nice to others if they push the buttons for the automatic doors to open, make room for people in wheelchairs on ramps and use the wheelchair accessible bathrooms only if no one else in the bathroom needs to use it.

One Christmas, Mom, Mark and I were shopping in the Brandon mall. We had been shopping for a while when Mom realized that it was time to change Mark's diaper. The three of us went into the public washrooms and found them to be very busy so we waited in line patiently. It was Mom and Mark's turn next so Mom started to get Mark out of his wheelchair. As Mom was doing that, a teenage girl standing behind me jumped in front of us and took the wheelchair accessible bathroom as another girl came out of it. We were extremely angry. There was no reason for that girl to jump ahead of us and take the washroom. She could see that we were next in line. Mom and Mark ended up having to wait for that girl to get out of that bathroom stall as the two of them could not get in the smaller cubicles. Two other girls and I ended up getting to use the washroom before Mom and Mark were able to use the wheelchair accessible bathroom.

As Mark's progress was slow, his IEP for the next school year, 1991-1992, remained similar to the year before. Mark's teacher and teacher assistants became more aware of his skills and purchased additional materials. Therapy putty was an item purchased to help strengthen Mark's fine motor skills. Therapy Putty is like Play-Doh except it is a lot stronger. In order to strengthen the fingers, students push and pull the putty to form different shapes or play a kind of tug a war with it.

Mark improved immensely in his receptive language. He began to understand and respond more consistently to things asked of him. He also started to be more familiar with routines of the classroom. A good example is the communication logbook that Mark carried back and forth between home and school. Mark could find his own logbook even if it was under something else on the teacher's desk.

Mark's health had improved. Mom no longer needed to blend all his food. Most foods he could eat normally except tough meat like roast beef. Unfortunately, in February 1992, Mark became ill again. He missed a total of 18 school days and was in the hospital again for a few days. He needed his esophagus dilated and was dehydrated from throwing up constantly. Mark recovered after three weeks, but it set him back on all his skills at school.

When a child with a disability reaches the age of fourteen, their school IEP's become ITP's or Individualized Transition Plans. These plans involve discussions about the student's future living arrangements and vocational abilities. These discussions are important for the classroom teacher as he/she can provide the child with opportunities to learn skills that he/she will need for their future life. At this time in the child's life, more agencies become involved. Community Service Workers (CSW) generally have been involved with the child since the very beginning, but often a change of workers takes place around their 18th birthday. At the age of 16, a CSW needs to start applying for funding from the government as their future living arrangements and day programs could be expensive. Vocational Rehabilitation Counsellors (someone who helps a person obtain and maintain employment) don't usually get involved until the student's last year of high school, but discussions can start much earlier.

Mom, Dad, and the Community Service Worker decided that it was time to think about Mark's future, as he was now fourteen. Mark could stay in school until he was 21 years of age. The Canadian and American governments have stated that a child with a disability has to be educated in their home school until they are 21 years of age. This basically is because the school divisions and the governments realize that children with special needs learn at a slower rate and are usually less mature than their counterparts. These four extra years help to close the gap and allow the students extra time to learn skills to function in everyday life. Most people spend an average of three to four years at college, university or trade school after they graduate from high school. Therefore, students with special needs actually have the same amount of schooling as most normal children. These extra years also give families a longer time to figure out what their child is going to do with his/her life.

Mom and Dad wanted to put Mark in a group home when he reached the age of 21. At that time there were two group homes in Virden with waiting lists. My parents decided to put Mark's name on the waiting list so when he was 21 a spot would be available. They also met with a group of parents who had children roughly the same age as Mark. Their goal was to possibly get the government or ACL, Association for Community Living, to build more group homes in the Virden area. The parents decided that by the time all their children reached the age to leave home, there would be very little room in current group homes. Another group home in our area was the solution.

Being only sixteen at the time, I didn't think Mark should go and live with a bunch of strangers. I wanted him to come and live with me when I had my own home. I realize now how unrealistic that was. Mark needed to be with his peers. He had to live his own life just like other people. The more I am involved with the special needs population the more I see the similarities in growing up rather than the differences. Group homes could be thought of as university dorms. Group homes are sometimes exactly what people with disabilities need and, to be honest, I think most eighteen year olds would benefit from the same type of situation. The individuals learn skills needed to take care of their own home. They learn how to cook, clean, pay bills, live with others, and develop money management skills. They also get to learn all of these while living with their peers. People of normal intelligence sometimes have to learn these skills on their own and sometimes it is a struggle. People with disabilities deserve to do things that normal peers would do like moving away from home. Moving away from home probably was what needed to be done when Mark reached 21 years of age. I just wasn't ready for him to grow up then and maybe I wasn't ready to grow up either.

For siblings of people with disabilities, adulthood creates a lot of mixed emotions. There is uncertainty about what their brother or sister's life might look like. When parents die or are too ill to take care of the child with a disability, the responsibility usually falls to the sibling. There can be resentment due to the added pressure of this type of responsibility. Unfortunately, this is an added pressure that some just can't deal with. For this reason, I think it's important for families to discuss the options that they have before the situation is upon them. It's a time for siblings to decide just how much responsibility they want to have. If they decide not to do it, the sibling may have to deal with feelings of guilt. If it's decided that the sibling will be responsible for the person's care, it's important that they become involved in the planning for their sibling's future as soon as possible. This may require that the sibling start attending meetings with the parents. It would be much easier to become involved before a tragedy happens.

I was starting to believe that people's attitudes were improving, but something happened to make me realize that the attitudes were still out there. Trent didn't seem to encounter as many problems as I had. Of course, I was oversensitive, as many of my friends will agree, and tended to get upset very quickly. Trent, on the other hand, would state his point and people would never say another word.

My dad was on the V.C.R.C. board (Virden Community Recreation Commission). This meant that he was on the Board of Directors that ran the skating rink and the swimming pool. Dad had always found it difficult to get Mark into the swimming pool because there were no large stairs for him to walk down and he was getting too big to carry. There were just little ladders in the water that were only big enough for one person and were hard for people with disabilities to use. The Board decided to buy a large staircase to put in the shallow end of the pool specifically for people with disabilities as well as the other patrons. The ladder worked wonderfully for all types of people and it was a good addition for the pool. One day when I was lifeguarding in the shallow end, I heard three young boys talking about the ladder. One of the boys asked the others what the ladder was for. One boy told him that the ladder was needed for the "retards" to get into the water because they were too stupid to use the other ladders. Needless to say, I couldn't just stand there and listen so

I explained as politely as possible that the stairs were needed for people with special needs because they needed extra help to get into the water not because they were stupid. By the time I was done explaining, I was so mad I was shaking.

I was very disappointed in the world's attitudes that day. It was obvious to me that those children had learned their attitudes from their parents, as they were not old enough to come up with comments like that. They had to have heard it somewhere. It is up to parents to teach their children about the wrongs of prejudice. If children grow up thinking that this attitude is okay they will continue to think that, but if we teach them that it is wrong they may learn to look at a person from the inside rather than the outside. It is a vicious cycle that I'm afraid will never be broken. Imagine what a peaceful world we could have if everyone learned to be tolerant of others.

CHAPTER 16

The 1992-1993 school year was my last year of high school. Trent was in grade five and Mark was fifteen years old. We were growing up fast and I was ready for the next stage in life.

Mom always felt that I would be a teacher. She said I tried to teach Mark things at home. She remembers me pretending to read to him when I was just three years old and maybe that was the beginning of my teaching career. When I was in grade six, the questions about our future careers started popping up. Our family went to Minot, ND for a holiday twice a year with the Lane family. I loved Minot and decided that I wanted to go to Minot State University and learn how to teach deaf people, as sign language had always fascinated me. Everyone said that I would change my mind a million times before I finally decided because most people do. It seems strange that I never changed my mind, and yet it was only natural for me to teach special needs children. In my grade twelve year, I decided that I wanted to be a special education teacher because I wanted to teach kids like Mark. I knew that I would still get to learn sign language because a lot of special needs children use it to communicate even if they aren't deaf. Now that I am a special education teacher I realize that it was my destiny. There is nothing else I would ever want to do.

Our school decided to offer a new course in my grade twelve year.

It was called cooperative work experience and consisted of students volunteering two hours every day at a work placement site that would give them insight into their future career. I decided that this class would be a great learning experience as well as give me a chance to spend more time with my brother. From February until April, I worked at Goulter Elementary School. I worked with two students with Down Syndrome, and one student who had very special needs. The two Down Syndrome students both used sign language, as their communication skills were limited. In fact it was one of them who gave me my name sign that I still use today. My name sign is the sign language letter "k" just below my neck. The student picked that because he liked my necklace. From April to June, I worked in my brother's life skills classroom. Those two hours were the best hours of every day. I not only saw my brother for two extra hours every day, but I saw the other side of Mark's life. I saw what hard work it took to teach him his skills. There were four other students in the room besides Mark so I was given a chance to work with them as well. Mark probably didn't enjoy it that much because I started making him practice his skills at home seeing as I knew the steps that they were teaching him. Who knows? Maybe he did enjoy it. Everyday before I left, I gave him a big hug.

One significant thing happened during that time. It is a memory that I have kept close to my heart every since. It always manages to bring tears to my eyes when I think of that special moment. One day at work experience, Mrs. Plaisier, Mark's teacher, thought it would be a great time to teach him the word "sister." We weren't really sure if he knew that I was his sister because he had never really given us a sign of understanding that concept before. The first day we were teaching him the new word, all the students and staff were standing up in the classroom getting ready to go to music class. Mark was standing by the classroom door and I was standing by the students' desks. Mrs. Plaisier asked him, "Where is your sister, Mark?" With a big grin on his face, he awkwardly ran straight towards me and almost knocked me over to give me one very special hug. I had never seen him move so fast. The tears welled up in my eyes as we were hugging. I was so happy I could barely speak. When we were done hugging, he stood back and started to giggle. It was as if he was trying to say, "see I'm not so dumb after all." There was not a dry eye in that classroom and when I went back to school that afternoon, I could barely tell my friends the story through my tears.

People had always questioned whether Mark really understood things or if he was just in his own little world. We defended him and felt that he could understand, but it was difficult to tell. I never knew for certain until that day how much he did comprehend. I always wondered if he even knew who I was and what I meant to him. I would have been quite sad if he didn't understand, but he did. He knew exactly who I was. That hug was the most significant hug I will ever receive and it is my most treasured memory.

Another event that occurred that year brings the opposite feeling when I think about it. One day my supervisor for the cooperative work experience class asked me, "Are you absolutely sure you want to do this for the rest of your life?" It wasn't so much the words he said, but it was the way he said them. He couldn't understand why I would want to teach kids who were so "stupid." He only wanted to teach the smart kids. The ones that could learn as he put it. He made it seem like children with disabilities were worthless and I was just as worthless for wanting to help them. I guess people who have never had the opportunity to know somebody with special needs may feel this because they don't know how to handle them.

Other times, people may be scared that it might rub off on them or that they might get hurt. These people are very ignorant in that they never ask questions about the person. They don't want to even know what that person's life is like. I often compare the situation to anything that makes people scared. Do eighteen year olds shy away from college because they are scared? Do people who want babies not have them because they are scared? Do we not get married because we are scared? The answer to these questions is usually no. People find a way to overcome their fears. They find information and read about it. In the same way people can overcome their fear or ignorance of people with special needs. They can read stories about people with disabilities. They can ask questions if they don't understand. They can spend time with someone with special needs. These are just a few of the many ways people can learn about people with disabilities.

In my classroom, I started a program called "Circle of Friends." I paired one of my special needs students with a regular high school student. Both individuals were unsure about what to expect from each other, but by the end of that first school year, they had each come away with a new perspective and a new friend. It was a wonderful experience for everyone involved and I have continued the program every year since. In a lot of ways those high school students were more mature and more compassionate than my supervisor will ever be. One example of how compassionate a young individual can be occurred during the planning of a school activity day. The Student Council president, also a Circle of Friends member, came to me before finalizing the plans for that particular day. She shared with me the plans that had been make to ensure that all my students would be able to participate fully in the activities. She did a bit of rearranging to make sure that my students would be fully included in the day as well as have fun participating in all the activities.

Again Mark became sick in the beginning of May 1993. On the Saturday morning of May long weekend (a common weekend for Mark to get sick), Mark became extremely ill. Time moved so slowly that day that I felt like I was in a daze. When we woke that morning, Mark was so cold he almost looked blue and his body seemed lifeless. He couldn't bear any weight on his legs or even hold his own head up. Dad tried to get him into the car himself, but no matter what angle he tried, Mark was just too heavy. Mom called our neighbour, Ken Clarke, who instantly came to help. Between the two of them they gathered Mark up and put him in our car. As soon as he was in his seat, Mom and I jumped into the car and left for the Brandon hospital. I watched Dad's face as we were driving out of the garage that day. It was a look that I vowed I never wanted to see again, but as life is not always kind, I have seen it far more often than I care to admit. He looked like he had just lost the most important thing in his life. He felt like he was seeing his son alive for the last time. That moment I realized that I needed to pray constantly the entire way to Brandon, which is a 77 km drive from our place. I tried to keep Mom's mind off of what was happening, but our conversation was strained. I listened to Mark's breathing all the way into Brandon. Mark would breathe and then it would seem like minutes before he would breath again. I never said anything to Mom because I knew she was worried enough without knowing her son was barely breathing. At that time I was training to become a National Lifeguard so I had taken first aid, CPR, and emergency care treatment. As I sat there listening for his breaths, I had it all figured out. I could give Mark mouth to mouth from where I was sitting very effectively if he needed it. I was running through the proper steps of doing artificial respiration as Mom and I were talking. I was also taking mental note of Mark's vitals such as the colour of his skin or the way his pupils were reacting to light. Neither Mom nor I had ever been so relieved to have arrived at our destination, as we were that morning. When we arrived at the emergency room, the doctor was waiting for us as Mom had called to say we were coming. The nurses wheeled Mark into a room while another nurse escorted us to the waiting room. We sat on ugly green benches that were extremely uncomfortable. I sat watching people come in and out of the big doors of the hospital. People were laughing and carrying on as if the world was great, but somewhere in one of those rooms, my little brother was fighting for his life. This hospital trip was not like our usual trips. I knew Mark was dying. I could see the signs as if there was a large sign in front of my face telling me it was true. Mom and I sat, each in our own thoughts, praying that it was going to be all right. Finally after about 15 minutes, the doctor came out looking very grim. Mark seemed to have an infection throughout his entire body. He had a very low maybe even non-existent blood pressure. His heart was racing and he was vomiting profusely. It seemed that his stomach was somehow paralysed. Nothing in his body seemed to be working properly. They were going to drain his entire body to get rid of the infection and the doctor said that they would do everything they could.

We called Dad to tell him what was happening and he and Trent were on the road within minutes. Again Mom and I found ourselves in the waiting room. Waiting to find out if someone you love is going to live or die is the most horrible thing to go through. It's like waiting to find out if you remember how to breathe. It's frustrating because there is nothing you can do, but sit, wait, and pray.

I always thought that my Mom was an amazing person. As a teenager, I would never have let her know that, but as we sat in the hospital waiting room that day, it became clear to me just how strong she truly was. There were very few times in our lives that I remember her crying. She just seemed to deal with situations as they happened. Maybe she cried when no one was around or she kept busy to keep her mind off the situation. That day, however, she was extremely quiet. There were still no tears, but I'm positive her heart was breaking.

About an hour later, the doctor came to tell us that Mark's right lung was a little asphyxiated. His kidneys were also failing and it was thought that he might need to have dialysis. He felt that the situation could worsen as he could become comatose. He currently seemed to be in a semi-coma state. This was a lot of information in a short time, but what could we do but take it all in?

It just didn't seem to be fair. Mark didn't deserve this. He never did anything wrong. I just didn't understand, but I continued to pray. By that afternoon our prayers were answered. Very slowly, he started to get better. I felt that everything was going to be okay so I agreed to leave the hospital with my boyfriend for a little while as Dad and Trent had arrived to be with Mom.

Being with my boyfriend of one year was what I thought I needed, but after an hour I realized that my life needed a change. It was as if my life flashed before my eyes in that hospital and I had changed in those few short hours. We went to a restaurant in Brandon for something to eat and it was while I was sitting there listening to him and one of his friends talk that I realized I didn't want to be his girlfriend anymore. They were talking about silly things. It was as if nothing serious had happened. But, for me, something had. My brother had almost died. I thought I was madly in love with this guy. It fact, we had even talked about getting married in the future. I realized that day that he really didn't know anything about me. He certainly didn't understand what my life was like. I always had a great way to scope people out. I let them meet Mark and from there I could figure out what kind of person they really were. Mark was a great judge of character. You could tell when he really liked someone and when he didn't. Often the people that he didn't like were those that didn't respect people like Mark. I surrounded myself with people who loved to spend time with Mark or listen to his stories as much as I did. Those were the people that I wanted near me. It never occurred to me until that day that this guy wasn't for me. He was truly a great guy who was very sweet and thoughtful and a part of me did love him. He cared about Mark and was good with him, but he didn't love him the way I did. I needed my boyfriend to love my family including Mark the way I did because otherwise it just wasn't going to work. I sometimes wonder if that was God's way of sending me a message. He made me see that my life needed a new direction.

    Mark spent a month in the hospital. His progress was slow, but it was consistent. I visited Mark quite a bit when he was in the hospital. Two of my friends, Fiona Lamont and Kara Morcombe, drove me down to see him one day. My close friends had always been supportive of Mark and my family. They weren't just there for me, but for my entire family. In fact, Trent spent a lot of time with my friends. Trent may have been a lot younger, but he managed to make them like spending time with him as well. I was taking my lifeguard course in Brandon every Monday night so I managed to spend an extra hour with Mark before classes. One evening I was reading a book to Mark when a nurse came in to check on him. She told me that I was a great sister for spending time with him. It was a nice compliment, but to me it was easy. I was his sister and he was my brother. I didn't need any other reason than that.

CHAPTER 17

The concept of time remains a mystery. Time appears to go slower when we are anticipating a huge event in our lives. And yet when our lives are full of joy and happiness, it moves so quickly that we seldom enjoy the special moments. If we could only stop time from disappearing on us, maybe then we could remember and appreciate every detail of those memories that return again and again to our inner vision.

The next year held wonderful moments as well as devastating experiences for our entire family. Everything about me changed in that year and I sometimes wonder if I even recognize the girl that I was back then. On April 28, 1993, I turned 18, which meant I was legally allowed to go to the bars in Manitoba. That was a wonderful feeling as it felt like I had finally grown up, yet it bothered me that Mark might not be able to have the same freedom. If he had been normal, he would have been able to obtain his license. It disturbed me that he didn't have friends like I did or wasn't able to go out and have fun like me. It never bothered him, though, because he didn't really know the difference. I had mentioned my concerns to some of my friends and they simply said that when Mark turned 18 they would take him to the bars. I realized instantly that they were being serious. They would definitely be there for Mark's 18th birthday and I started to look forward to that day.

Mark actually liked to drink beer. Just because he wasn't 18 didn't mean that he'd never had a drink. Dad allowed Mark to have some beer whenever he was drinking. One Christmas Dad gave him some beer in front of my Grandma Leslie. She is very strict and didn't approve of alcohol. She takes life pretty seriously and I think she thought her family should always act appropriately. My grandma couldn't believe that Dad would give Mark alcohol and she got very upset with him. Dad simply replied, "Normal kids his age do it so why can't he?"

In June of 1993, I met my future husband, Scott Smith. We started spending a lot of time together. We had a lot of the same friends so we ended up at the same parties on weekends. I enjoyed his company and thought he was a really great friend, but it never once occurred to me that it would become anything serious. When I realized he liked me, I never really thought about liking him back. I wasn't looking for anything serious. I just wanted to enjoy my last few months before going to university. I look back on it now and realize how blind I really was. I thank Mark and my friends for showing me what I was missing.

My graduation from high school came and went in the blink of an eye. Mark only came for our family pictures, as he couldn't have sat through the ceremony. It would have been nice if he could have come to the dance, but Mom and Dad felt it wasn't the right place for him. Some people probably wouldn't have accepted him there anyway. It's too bad because Mark and I loved music and we would have enjoyed dancing together. I would often go into his room and dance with him to whatever song he was listening to. At Grandpa and Grandma Hayward's 50th wedding anniversary dance Mark and I danced many times before he had to go home. We had so many people looking at us and smiling. Someone came up and told me I was a great sister, but this statement bothered me for wasn't I just dancing with my brother like any other sister does?

I went away to university in Minot, North Dakota that fall. It was extremely hard to move away from my family and friends. It was a bit easier to become separated from my friends as we were all moving in different directions, but moving away from my family was extremely hard. We were very close because of all we'd been through. One of my friends told me that you could feel the love when you walked into our house. I never noticed it, but I guess it was there. I missed talking with my parents. I missed arguing with Trent, but most of all I missed confiding in Mark. I missed his laughter, his hugs, and his smile. I even missed his screaming and crying. Mark missed me a lot, too. Mom had hung a picture of me in his room so he could look at me anytime he wanted. Often, Mom would come into his room and he would be standing there staring at my picture.

Those first few months were hard, but I had lots of support. I found some good friends (Tammy Swanson, for one, who I now consider a best friend) in Minot and talked to at least one family member or friend everyday. I also talked to Scott every night. Within a few short months, he had become my best friend. It didn't occur to me that I talked to him more than I did my actual boyfriend at the time or that I could be more myself when with him. As the months continued, after several honest discussions with my closest friends, I finally realized that I had fallen in love with Scott. Everyone else had figured it out long before I did. I think even Mark knew. He always seemed to giggle when I mentioned Scott's name. In December of 1993, we made it official and started dating.

Scott was already acquainted with my family and I soon came to realize that Mark loved Scott and that he was amazing with Mark. Scott didn't seem to see the disability. He knew exactly how to handle him. Scott teased him like crazy and Mark loved it. One night in February Scott said to me, "You know, Kim, we don't have to go out all the time. (We spent most weekends out with friends.) We could baby-sit Mark and let your parents go out. I'm sure they need a break once in awhile." I just turned and stared at him. I couldn't believe it! Nobody had ever said anything like that to me before. No guy had ever offered to baby-sit Mark with me. No guy had ever thought that maybe my parents needed a break. I knew at that moment that he cared about my family as much as I did and I had found my soul mate.

In February of 1994 Mark was sick, but this time it didn't last long. He was in the hospital for only one weekend. He was extremely restless and didn't seem to want to be there. It was as if he knew he had something more important to do. Little did we know, he seemed to sense something that we didn't. He wanted to be home!

Scott and I started spending more time at home looking after Mark or spending time with my family. Scott would help me feed Mark. He would help me change him, put him to bed and play with him. The two of them liked to tease me. Scott would say something funny about me and Mark would giggle. Who knows if Mark understood what Scott was saying or if he just loved the attention. Mark had a miniature shuffleboard game that they used to play together. They also had a game that they played with a clothespin which actually in a way helped strengthen Mark's fine motor skills. Scott would attach the clothespin to Mark's shirt. Mark would then grab the clothespin and give it back to Scott to continue the game. If I asked Mark to give me the clothespin, he wouldn't. He would start laughing and give it to Scott. He thought that was a great game!

My life seemed to be complete. I was living all my dreams and was very happy. I was attending Minot State University to become a special education teacher. I was surrounded by amazing friends who pushed and supported me to reach my goals. I found the man of my dreams. My family was happy and healthy. It was perfect, though I've come to believe that perfection doesn't last forever.

Ever since I was a little girl, I had nightmares about Mark dying. It probably started with Mark's first trip to the hospital. I realized that the possibility of his dying was a reality even though I didn't want to face that. We just didn't know when it was going to happen. Maybe I never expected it to really happen. When I started university, the nightmares got worse. I thought that it was just because I missed him, but now I look back and realize I should have seen the signs. By Easter, the nightmares were happening every night. I never mentioned them to anyone, not even Scott.

A week after Easter, Mark became ill again. This time it didn't seem too bad because he didn't need to go to the hospital. That whole week, I lost a great deal of sleep. I was lucky if I fell asleep before 3:00 am and even then it was a very restless sleep. The nightmares were endless and very detailed. The night of Trent's 12th birthday,

April 7, I called to wish him a happy birthday. Mom let me talk to Mark for a minute on the phone. His version of talking was just listening to me babble. When Mom got back on the phone, I asked her how Mark was doing. She said he seemed fine except he couldn't keep anything down. In fact, he had thrown up a piece of something that kind of looked like a grasshopper. They weren't really sure what it was, but they were going to see Mark's doctor first thing the next morning. I was coming home the next day for the weekend because I was starting figure skating lessons again so we decided to talk the next day. After I got off the phone, a very uneasy feeling overcame me but I couldn't put my finger on it. I had another nightmare that night. When I awoke, it was storming outside and I started to wonder if I was going to get home. The next morning it was really storming. There was snow everywhere. I called my parents and they thought I should stay in Minot, but I was determined to come home. Another girl was catching a ride with me so we decided to go out on the road and see how bad it really was. No roads had been closed so it couldn't be too bad. We realized pretty quickly that the roads weren't good. For some reason I knew I had to get home so turning around was never an option. It took us four long hours when it should only have taken two. When we got to town, I dropped my friend off and headed for Grandpa and Grandma Hayward's to tell them I had arrived home safely as my parents were at the hospital in Brandon. I was supposed to skate that afternoon, but it was cancelled due to the storm so I went home. When I got there, my parents had just gotten home themselves. Mark had to stay at the hospital, but he seemed to be feeling better so they decided to come home for the night. Around 7:30 p.m. one of the nurses called to say that Mark seemed really upset and they couldn't settle him down. She wondered if someone could come in and sit with him. Dad wasn't feeling very well so he stayed home to look after Trent and his friend that had come to celebrate his birthday. Mom and I decided that we would go in.

I had listened to the phone call from the nurse and I got the feeling that Mark needed me. I didn't really understand the odd feeling I was having. I felt his pain and seemed to know that he needed me to be there. I knew something was seriously wrong. I had made arrangements to stay at my friends' apartment and Mom would stay at the hospital. I called Scott and told him where I would be. That was the only night he had off from work so we figured we wouldn't see each other that weekend. Mom and I left Virden around 9:00 PM and Brandon is roughly a 45 minute drive. The storm had cleared up a bit, but the roads still weren't great. I remember looking at the clock in my car around 9:30 p.m. and a sad feeling came all over my body. I never said anything to Mom, but I knew something was happening that was going to change our lives.

We got off the elevator on the children's ward around 10:00 PM. The ward seemed to have a strange feel to it. It was very dark and felt like someone was mourning. We went to go into Mark's room when one of the nurses stopped us. As I looked into her eyes, I knew what had happened. I just didn't admit it to myself. She told us that Mark's heart had stopped around 9:30. The exact time that strange feeling had overtaken me. The doctors did everything they could to save him, but his heart just gave up.

I was in complete shock. I didn't seem to understand what she was saying even though I should have known exactly what she meant. The nurse led Mom and I to the children's playroom. I had spent hours in that very room watching videos with Mark, reading him books, and playing games with him. I looked around the room remembering those times so clearly. The nurse asked if we would like a minister to sit with us. I immediately said yes so the nurse left to find the minister. I then turned and asked Mom what she meant. Quietly, in clear definite words, she told me that Mark had died. Instantly I burst into tears and so did Mom. We sat crying for a while before the nurse came back and asked if we would like to make some phone calls. Mom made the hardest call she'll ever have to make. She called to tell Dad. Trent had picked up the other extension and overheard Mom tell Dad that Mark had died. They didn't know that he was on the phone, but as soon as Mom said the word "dead," a loud shrilling scream was heard. Dad and Trent instantly headed to Brandon. I then tried to track Scott down. I called all over, but couldn't get hold of him. Everyone must have thought I was crazy to be calling so late. I never told anyone what had happened, just that I needed him right then. Because I couldn't find Scott, I called my friends' house. Brenda answered the phone and I instantly blurted out what had happened. I don't think she even said good-bye. She just said she'd be there in five minutes. That was the way my friends were. It didn't matter what they were doing or what time it was, they were always there for me. I'm glad she did because she knew exactly how to handle the situation. She just walked into the room, hugged my mom, and then held my hand. No words were necessary. People seem to think that in tragic times like death they have to say something remarkable or inspiring. In reality, silence speaks volumes.

While we waited for everyone to come, the nurse asked if we wanted to see Mark. Mom didn't want to, but I did. I walked into the cold, dark room. It had a light on, but it still seemed dark to me. In fact, the light looked more heavenly than anything. Mark was lying there on the hospital bed. He looked as if he was just sleeping. He had no tubes attached to him and no machines were visible. He was just lying there with his favourite toy, Bugs Bunny. As I looked closer, I could see that there was no movement at all. He really was dead. I grabbed his hand and held it for a really long time as my tears leaked out and in that moment my heart broke into a million tiny pieces. I could feel his hand growing colder in mine. As I stared at his lifeless body, the memories of all the time we shared whirled around my head. I just kept hoping that this was another dream. It had to be. It was like the others, so detailed and so vivid. It couldn't be truly happening. I thought I would eventually wake up, but I didn't. It was real this time. He was really gone. And then I remembered the song I used to sing to Mark at bedtime. I sang it whenever he needed comforting. The song never meant anything to me before. I just used it because I knew all the words and I could actually sing it not too badly. Ironically, the song now fit the situation. As I held his hand in mine and tears stained my face, I very quietly started to sing "*You Are My Sunshine*" written by Jimmie Davis and Charles Mitchell. When

I finished singing, I leaned over and took his Bugs Bunny. As I walked out that door with the nurse's arm around me, I knew my sunshine would never be as bright as it was with him. For the first five days after Mark's death, Bugs Bunny never left my side except when I showered. Since then it has traveled with me everywhere and will continue to for the rest of my life. It is an everlasting symbol of my best friend.

When I went back to the waiting room, Brenda was still there. I gave her a huge hug as we mourned together. Shortly after that, Scott and his best friend, Terry Williams, showed up at the hospital. They had been coming into Brandon to see me, but they hadn't expected to find the situation they did. They both hugged me tight and then sat with us. Brenda was on one side and Scott on the other side each holding a hand. Dad and Trent finally arrived with Bob and Linda Lane. Dad figured he couldn't drive by himself so naturally he called his best friends. Dad wanted to see Mark so Bob and he went in to say good-bye while Linda sat to comfort my mom. I had never seen my father cry. He has always been extremely strong, but that night he cried for the part of him that was lost forever.

Around midnight we left the hospital. Mom, Dad, Trent, Bob, and Linda went home while Scott, Terry, Brenda, and I went to see our friends. A bunch of my other close friends were at the apartment when we got there, but I don't really remember anything else. It was like I was walking in my own body and yet my heart was somewhere else. Finally, Scott and I drove home in silence. He just held my hand while I cried silently beside him. I remember staring out at the darkened night. There weren't even any stars to wish upon. I didn't know what to do or what to say. I just wanted to die myself. My heart hurt so badly that I actually thought I was going to die. Never before had the world seemed so dark, gloomy and unfair. When we got home, a lot of my aunts, uncles, and cousins were there to comfort us. There was a strangeness to our home that I had never felt before. Everyone was busy talking and eating. On occasion it was silent, but then someone started talking again. They discussed the weather, or what they had been doing that night or what was going on in the world. I just didn't understand how they could discuss such meaningless things. I felt like the world had stopped, but it just seemed to kept going full speed ahead.

We finally went to bed around 4 am, but I couldn't sleep. I tossed and turned. My life was never going to be the same again and I didn't know how I was going to go on. What was I going to do without Mark?

The next few days were filled with family, friends and lots of emotions. Certain events stand out in my mind, but most of it is still a daze. Bob and Linda were at our house constantly taking care of meals, phone calls, and guests. They also managed to get each of us out of the house every once in a while. Grandpa and Grandma Hayward were there first thing the next morning. Grandma Hayward cries at the drop of a hat so you can just imagine the state she was in. Grandpa and Grandma Leslie were there shortly after that as well, trying to find comfort in people's visits. Aunts, uncles, and cousins were constant visitors for the next few days. Auntie Myrna from Portland flew down and brought a smile to my dad's face. Throughout the whole ordeal friends and family surrounded us. My friends were pretty amazing. They all came and spent time with Trent or me. They got Trent out of the house once in a while and tried to help whenever they could. My parents had to make a lot of decisions about the funeral. Until you have to organize a funeral, you have no idea how hard or how expensive it is. They had to pick flowers, a coffin, songs for the service, what he would be dressed in, and the list just went on and on. Mom thought that she could pick the flowers for Mark's coffin, but she had made so many other decisions that day that she couldn't handle any more. In the end Brenda and I went to the flower shop to decide, but to be honest it was Brenda that finally made the decision as I didn't really want to think about Mark being in a coffin let alone putting flowers on it. Our minister, Reverend Brenda Ferguson, came to our house to discuss songs, which was probably the one area where I knew exactly what was needed. It was all totally devastating. It was the hardest five days of our lives, but little did I realize those were just the beginning of the hard days.

Everything was so surreal. It felt more like a dream than reality.

Mark's viewing and a simple family service were held on Tuesday evening at the funeral home. Reverend Trevor Rutley gave the service. He was retired but had been our childhood minister and knew Mark well. I'll never forget seeing Mark lying in his coffin. All I could do was cry as I looked at the toys we put in with him like his small music keyboard and his A&W Bear. He looked so peaceful, but that thought didn't comfort me. I was one of the first people to walk in to the viewing room. Everyone else followed. Dad put his arms around me as if trying to shield me from the pain I was feeling inside. Grandpa Leslie reached over the church pew and held my hand ever so gently. Even though they were grieving just as much as I was, they found the inner strength to reach out and comfort me. As the service continued, my tears gradually ceased, but I knew my heart would never feel complete again.

After the service, hugs and more tears were shed among the family members. Every member of our extended family was there as well as Mark's teacher. My cousins held me tight with each hug. They were feeling my sadness, but they couldn't take it away. My pain was just too deep. All they could do was be there, and that they were. After awhile I went back in to say one last good-bye to Mark and I found Scott standing by himself crying. Even though he had only known Mark for a few short months, his pain was just as evident as the rest of my family. Maybe even more because he felt so helpless. There was nothing he could do to ease the pain our family was feeling.

Wednesday morning a funeral service for the entire community was held. Craig and Corey Lane were the ushers so I saw them first when I entered the church, but I couldn't even make eye contact with them. As we walked to our seats, I could feel everyone's eyes on me. Maybe it was because I was carrying Bugs Bunny, but whatever it was, it wasn't comforting even though I knew they were all there to share our grief. Seeing his coffin and the flowers was enough to make me want to run screaming out the door. All I could do was cry. I remembered all the wonderful memories that we shared and realized there would be no more. As the service went on my tears started to cease. I seemed to have forgotten my faith in the last few days. I was angry with God for taking Mark away from our family. I just couldn't understand how he could take this great person away. He had never done anything to hurt anyone. He embodied what I thought God wanted us to be. He loved unconditionally and was the kindest, most gentle person I knew. I just didn't get it, but as Reverend Ferguson started her sermon, I realized that Mark would no longer be in pain. Mark would find his voice in heaven. He would be able to run and jump, as he never had on earth. He would no longer be teased and ridiculed, but he also would no longer be with his family. "In God's new world Mark is able to run and walk. Imagine what it must be like for him today, a new world, all kinds of places to explore and many people to love, people who love him like we do" (Ferguson, B., 1994). Reverend Ferguson's sermon was beautiful. She always used stuffed animals to help children understand the sermons and on this day it was very appropriate. She used Trent's teddy bear that was given to him by Grandpa and Grandma Hayward that Christmas. "Because God has sent Jesus Christ into our world and because Jesus spoke about God so very much we know that there is another world beyond this one. In that world this Christmas bear, Trent's own bear, would be what we would see. Isn't he beautiful now, with all these fine colours? He is bigger and brighter. He is free from all pain and sickness. We believe that this is what has happened with Mark as well" (Ferguson, B., 1994). The entire service was directed more at all the children in the church rather than the adults. Children have a difficult time understanding death, where adults know that in life, death is only natural.

Linda Lane gave a special remembrance of Mark during the service. Dad was holding himself together as he comforted Mom, Trent and me. But as Linda mentioned Mark's enjoyment of riding with his Dad in the tractor, Dad burst into tears and started to shake. At that moment I realized just how hard this was for my parents. I could never understand their pain. No one loved Mark the way they did, and in dealing with my pain I forgot theirs. They were saying good-bye to their son.

Music was a special part of our family. When we were organizing the funeral, I knew instantly what song needed to be sung or maybe what song we needed to hear. The first time I heard the song "Wind Beneath my Wings" performed by Bette Midler and written by Larry Henley and Jeff Silbar, I felt like the song was written for Mark. Every word of it was how I felt about Mark.

When I heard a neighbour of my parents, Bev Eilers, singing this song at the funeral, I realized that my wind was gone. He now lived in heaven with God and all the others who had passed away before him. I struggled with that for a long time because I wanted him here and not in heaven. It took me a long time to realize that Mark is at peace and he will always be with me to guide my wings.

After the funeral, we drove out to the cemetery. Scott drove our car directly behind the hearse. When we crossed the highway, a police officer was there directing traffic with his lights and sirens going. Dad figured that Mark would have loved the lights and sirens. At the cemetery, Trent and I each placed a red rose on his coffin along with a white one. As we placed the flowers on the coffin, I remember thinking that this was where Mark was now. It was only a few miles from our farm so we could visit as much as we wanted. Today Mark's tombstone bears a picture of him, a music staff with notes for his love of music, and a stalk of wheat for his love of the farm. It has the dates of his life and a special quote that Scott helped me write. "His smile brightened our lives" and that it did. The world seems so gloomy now without his beautiful smile.

The events of those few days unfolded in front of my eyes, yet I felt as if I wasn't really seeing the whole picture. Those days were the hardest and most painful that we will ever encounter. When a member of the immediate family dies, a part of each member dies with him. Our family was no different except for the fact that Mark needed more love and more care than the average person, so his presence would be missed that much more. My heart shattered into a million pieces the day Mark died. Each piece flowed in different directions so I had no idea how to find them. Maybe I never will.

CHAPTER 18

One of my closest friends once told me that I could always find a silver lining in any cloud. The cloud of Mark's death hovered over me for many, many years. It blurred my senses so I couldn't find the silver lining for a long time. Those first few months after Mark's death are a big mystery to me. I don't really remember living at all. It just seemed that I floated through the motions of life.

The time following the death of a loved one is a very difficult time. Everyone has different experiences and different ways of dealing with their sadness. That first year following Mark's death was extremely difficult for us. Every holiday or celebration came with memories of past ones. Every mealtime, every weekend, and our daily routines brought sadness as we remembered what Mark would have done had he still been with us. Even though there were the four of us (Mom, Dad, Trent, and me) going through this difficult time, we each had to go through the journey on our own. We each reached different stages of grief at different times, which made it difficult to help each other. Even though we were there for each other and had lots of friends and family for support, it still was a very lonely and sad time.

Dad discovered he had diabetes shortly after Mark's death. He concentrated on becoming healthier, but at times it seemed he didn't really care. The will to live had died with Mark and to him life just wasn't the same anymore. Over the years the life in him has come back, but I know that in the privacy of his tractors, he still sheds tears for Mark. Today Dad is the one who keeps Mark's memories alive. He continues to tell the beloved stories of Mark's life. We now manage to laugh at the stories without shedding tears.

Mom found she had more time on her hands than she knew what to do with. Mark's room remained untouched for two years because she just couldn't find the strength to put his stuff away. For the longest time, she wouldn't even look at photographs of Mark. It was just too painful. She threw herself into crafts, sewing, gardening, and decorating the house. Four years after Mark died, she found a job at a store in Virden to keep her busy. Mom still has trouble talking about Mark and seems to worry more about her family. She does, however, discuss my job and gives me great insight into my students' lives. Maybe that is a way for her to keep Mark's memory alive.

As Trent was only twelve when Mark passed away, he grew up really fast. He bottled up all his feelings, but they were always right below the surface ready to snap at a moment's notice. He became more mature in some ways as a result of the tragedy. He found it difficult to connect with peers and began spending more time with people older than him. Trent began to experience difficulties in school and eventually had a reputation as a "bad boy." Trent has slowly began looking for help and we provided the support that he needed. He feels that he has now moved on and isn't really sure how it affected his life as he was very young. Mom, Dad, and I feel that Mark's death did affect his life, but we hope that he has truly moved on.

Being lonely was the hardest thing for me to learn to deal with. I can be in a room full of hundreds of people who are laughing and having a great time and still have a feeling of complete loneliness overtake any other feeling at that present time. I have come to realize that kind of loneliness can crop up anytime or anywhere, and especially when you least expect it. I don't think people can truly understand what it is like to be completely lonely until they sit in a room with five of their closest friends and have it overwhelm them to the point that they feel they can't even breathe. For me, that happened often those first few years. As time went on, I felt like that feeling would eventually go away. Unfortunately, it still seems to take me by surprise at the best of times. All you want to do is be with the one who is missing from your life, but knowing that you can't creates emotions inside that are so conflicting they are hard to explain. Throughout the years, as others from my life pass on, that loneliness continues to rear its ugly head.

The first week back to university, one of my best friends, Erin Brown, came with me and helped keep my head above water. I continued to come home every weekend for the duration of that school year. Home was where I needed to be. My parents decided that I might as well continue my skating lessons to keep my mind off Mark's death. My coach, my cousin Janelle Hodson, and Scott kept my focus on my skating while on the ice. I had been working on passing my gold dances for two years and had just one left to pass. I will never forget skating that gold dance on test day. It was the most amazing feeling I have ever had on ice. I decided before I even stepped on the ice that this time I was skating for Mark. That day I seemed to float as I was skating. It felt like there was a higher power out there with me and maybe there was. Maybe Mark was there watching and helping me. In the end, I had never skated that dance better and it paid off because I ended up passing my gold dance. That was the first moment after Mark's death when I realized that even though he was gone from earth he was very much here with me.

The last twelve years have been trying for my family, but through the sorrow I have found my silver lining. I found the most amazing man to spend the rest of my life with. It's interesting that Scott appeared in my life only a few short months before Mark's death. I always could judge what kind of people my friends were by the way they treated Mark. None of my previous boyfriends had ever given Mark a second glance and that is probably why they didn't remain in my life. Scott, on the other hand, cared very deeply about Mark and the rest of my family. I constantly think that Mark knew he could pass away because Scott would take care of our family. Mark could tell just what a special person Scott was long before the rest of us. Scott became a brother to Trent and another son to my parents long before he became my husband. Scott became my confidante, the shoulder to cry on, the hand that wiped the tears, the laughter through my tears, and my best friend. I knew that he was the one God meant for me to marry. He seemed to fill the void that Mark had left. On May 3, 1995, Scott asked me to marry him and, of course, I said yes. After a two-year wait until I completed my education degree, our wedding day finally came on July 12, 1997. As a little girl, I had always dreamed of Mark standing up for my husband. I pictured one of my friends either walking him up the aisle or pushing him in his wheelchair. He would have his Bugs Bunny toy so he didn't start to fuss during the service. I guess that dream wasn't going to be a reality.

We had planned an outdoor wedding much to my parents' dismay. They were petrified that they would go to all the hard work of fixing up the yard only to have it pour rain. I, on the other hand, knew that I had a guardian angel in heaven that would give us sunshine. Around 8:00 the morning of our wedding day, it started to pour and it didn't seem to want to let up. Everyone was coming to me asking if the wedding was going to be moved to the church. I kept insisting that it would eventually stop. Deep down I was worried, but I wasn't going to let anyone know that. Finally around 1:00 pm the rain stopped. It still was kind of dreary out, but at least the rain had stopped. The wedding was held at 3:00 pm and the most amazing thing happened as my Dad and I started to walk down the aisle. As Dad and I stepped up to the archway, the sun broke through the clouds. At that moment, I felt Mark's presence. He may not have been there in body, but his spirit was certainly felt within my heart. To me that was the biggest sign that I have ever gotten that our guardian angel is watching over us. I still believe that the rain that day was Mark's tears from heaven and the sun was his way of sharing our happiness.

Moving on has been tough for our family. There have been moments when we didn't think we could find the strength to carry on, and other moments that told us we had no choice. Mark wouldn't have wanted us to give up so we keep fighting for our hearts to become whole. With each ounce of strength we find, we slowly sew the pieces of our delicate hearts together. We find each piece in different places through the support of our families and friends, but we have come to realize that no matter how many pieces we find, there will always be holes within our hearts.

CHAPTER 19

Mark was silenced by fate, and yet his silence taught us how to truly listen. We learned to appreciate life and deal with death. We learned to be thankful for our many blessings—especially Mark's life. It's been twelve years since his death and not a day goes by that I don't think about his influence on our lives. We were all changed by his life and his death. I sometimes wonder where our family would be without Mark's presence. As my adult years continue on, I wonder what the future might have held for Mark's adulthood.

An adult with a mental disability requires more planning, more resources and more people involved than the average person. Mark had a Community Service Worker from the moment his disability was diagnosed. At the age of sixteen, the school division would have completed the necessary paperwork referring him to the Adult Community Service Worker. Community Service Workers need adequate time to complete the necessary paperwork to apply for government funding for the adult with special needs. Part of the paperwork involves making sure a current intellectual assessment has been given to the student. To be eligible for different services, the assessments must show a particular IQ score. Over the years, different professionals assessed Mark, but an IQ score could never be determined due to his lack of communication. Even though an IQ score was never found, his score would definitely have been below 70 or the magical number for certain services. It is important to note that services and resources can vary depending on where the individual lives.

Child and Family Services offers two programs, Supported Living and Day Services that can provide assistance to adults with mental disabilities. The Supported Living option can start as early as eighteen, but generally depends on the need for a change in the current living arrangements. Most parents start looking into this program between the ages of sixteen and eighteen so that the student is able to live away from home by the time they are twenty-one years of age. In the Supported Living program there are three main options. An adult can either live at the home of immediate or extended family members, own a home or apartment, or live in a private or agency run residential care facility. Depending on where the adult decides to live, the Community Service Worker will provide a worker for a specific amount of time each week to assist the adult in independent living skills such as banking and cooking skills. In a residential care facility, workers are there around the clock to provide assistance in their living skills. Mom and Dad were already looking into placing Mark in a group home before his death so I'm sure he would have lived in a residential care facility with 24-hour care as he could not have looked after himself.

The Day Services option starts after a student has graduated from high school at the age of twenty-one. Government funding does not start until after the student's twenty-first birthday. However, some school divisions and private agencies that provide day services have been known to make financial arrangements before this if the school setting is not working for the student. In the Day Services program, workers assist the adult in finding and maintaining a job, providing on-site support and job training and assist in teaching the adult job-related skills in a community setting or day service facility. Mark probably would have spent his days in a community facility known as Bridge Street. He would have been taught to do very simple, repetitive type tasks. Unlike some adults, Mark could not have found a job in the community due to his mental and physical abilities.

Another organization in Manitoba that provides services to help individuals obtain and maintain employment is Vocational Rehabilitation Services, although Mark probably would not have used this service. To be eligible for this program the student has to be over sixteen years of age and have either an intellectual (IQ less than 80), psychiatric, learning or physical disability. Teachers or the student's case manager refer the student to this program in their last year of high school by completing paperwork. Again the paperwork involves making sure the student has an up to date intellectual assessment. The student usually begins working with the vocational counsellor six months prior to graduation. Once the individual is considered eligible, a counsellor puts the student through a battery of vocational type tests. It takes a student between four and five ½ days to complete the computerized tests and work samples. From these tests, a counsellor creates a report explaining the student's strengths, weaknesses and possible work placements. The team then draws up an employment plan, but the individual is responsible for the majority of the planning. Often the vocational counsellor will help the student find an appropriate work placement. A job coach can then be hired to train the person. After a length of time, if the placement is working for both the individual and the company, the placement can be turned into either part or full time employment.

Unfortunately, people with moderate or severe disabilities have difficulty finding part or full time employment. Often businesses are willing to pay them for a few hours a day, but as their work skills are limited, employers are rarely willing to offer them more. Sometimes the people with disabilities aren't even paid minimum wage for their employment and therefore have difficulty making ends meet without some type of assistance. The Income Assistance for Persons with Disabilities program provides additional financial assistance for adults with a disability. In order to apply for this program, the individual must be eighteen, a resident of Manitoba and fill in an application. The application usually requires documentation of an intellectual assessment, as their IQ scores must be below a certain level. The person then has a meeting with a government official to determine eligibility for the program. Once a person is eligible, he/

she starts receiving financial assistance from the government. The amount he/she receives depends on the individual's employment. Mark would have been eligible for this program and the financial assistance would have been his only income.

When I was planning my adult years, it never once occurred to me to write a plan, but for Mark's adult years, a detailed plan would have been the only strategy. Just like the IEP process in education, adults with disabilities still require teams that plan their adult years. The IPP (individualized program plan) basically focuses on residential and vocational areas. The plan usually involves the individual's idea of his/her life and the steps needed to get him/her there. There are many different ways to collect and share information to create a plan with all team members. Personal Futures Planning, the Map process, Lifestyle Planning, Gathering Together and PATH are all examples of different techniques to create plans for adults with disabilities. PATH (Planning Alternative Tomorrows with Hope) is the most commonly used strategy today. In the PATH process, the adult starts by stating their dream or "The North Star." Once the dream is stated, the team sets a focus for the next year including where the adult is now and the people who are or need to be involved. Then the team discusses ways to help the adult build strengths over the next year which becomes the plan for the individual.

All the mentioned programs require decision-making on the part of the individual with special needs. Unfortunately, in the past, some decisions have been made by other people rather than the adult with special needs. Sometimes these decisions have caused a great deal of harm to the individual. On October 4, 1996 The Vulnerable Persons Living with a Mental Disability Act was passed. It is designed to protect the rights of people with mental disabilities who need assistance to meet their needs. The act is designed to make sure that people with mental disabilities are not being taken advantage of and to make sure they have a say in their life decisions. When a person with mental disabilities is unable to make decisions, a substitute decision maker (SDM) may be appointed. Supported decision-making means vulnerable persons making their own decisions with the support and advice from family and friends, if desired. Mark would have needed a SDM to help make all his decisions. The SDM has to complete an application to the Vulnerable Persons' Commissioner and be deemed eligible. Once eligible the person then has the responsibility to make decisions for that particular person. Often times the SDM is only allowed to make decisions in certain areas of the person's life and generally for only a certain amount of time. An SMD can be a parent, other family member, friend or any other person that can make decisions in the best interest of the individual.

On November 18, 2002, Scott and I entered a new phase of our lives—parenthood. Motherhood has changed my perspective of the world and given me a whole new sense of life's special gifts. My past life is now seen through a mother's eyes rather than a sister's and with that comes a new appreciation for my parents' strength and courage.

Our son's birth was long, difficult and ended in a caesarean section. At one point during labour I could sense everyone's anxiety, but at the same time I felt Mark's presence in the room. Maybe I had too many drugs in my system, but I truly could feel him there. I'm not sure I could explain the feeling that overcame me even if I tried, but maybe it was a little bit like dying for I felt a sense of total peace even though there was so much pain. It was as if Mark lent me his strength when I needed it the most. When our son was born, we instantly knew his name. It seemed only appropriate to name him Declan Marcus after his uncle. After Declan was born, I had a new appreciation for Mark's strength. Mark was often in so much pain and yet never complained. He spent great amounts of time in the hospital and yet seemed completely happy.

Declan's birth brought back memories of Mark's birth for my parents. Dad remembered the moments directly after his birth. It took Mark a long time to start breathing. The nurses had tried everything to get him to breathe, and finally they poured cold water on him. He then started to breathe. Mom and Dad had obviously suppressed some of this memory, but it seems more and more likely that his first few moments of life probably caused his disability. With this newfound knowledge, I feel more at peace—all those years of wondering if I had caused his disability. That peace makes me realize even more that Mark's life was not an accident, but more likely fate.

From the moment Declan was born, I could see Mark staring back at me. Most people don't see it or maybe people don't want to say it because they think it would be an insult and maybe I only see it because I want to see it, but I know a little piece of Mark's spirit lives inside Declan. Declan's eyes light up the way Mark's did and he has certain looks that are reminiscent of Mark. In certain photographs, their images definitely share a likeness, but it's his love of music and his fighting spirit that are most like Mark's soul. As Declan grows, Mom and Dad are reminded of memories of Mark's life that were once forgotten to shield the pain. However as Declan grows, his accomplishments will be more than Mark's and with that there will be no memories to compare.

They say that time heals all wounds, but I think time just patches the heart to make it easier to continue. Just like a patch on a pair of jeans, a single event can cause it to fray and open the wound to the familiar pain. One day Dad and I were watching Declan play with his toys. Dad looked at me and asked, "What do you think Mark would have thought of Declan?" And with that question, the loosely sewn threads that held the patch over my heart were once again broken into a million pieces. "I guess we will never know."

The memories of my brother will forever haunt my dreams. And it seems that as time goes on those pieces of him are slowly slipping one by one farther away from me. It is almost to the point where I wonder if the memories even happened at all, but I know that they are real. It always seems that it is the little things that I remember the most. I can never have him back in my life again no matter how hard I pray. I could never find anyone as special to replace him. He was my best friend in the whole world. When the world had shut me out, he was there. No one can truly understand the bond that we shared and the bond that I still carry in my heart. I can still feel his presence with me everyday, and no matter where life takes me, he will always be in my heart.

I pray that someone someday will come into everyone's life and affect them as Mark affected ours. I hope that time will allow us to see the difference people can make in our lives. Someday, Mark and I will meet again in the windows of heaven, but for now I have to be satisfied that his story of courage and survival will live on long after those that knew him best have left this world behind.

Every life has a story. The story is the journey of their lives. Some people's journeys are happy and wonderful while others are a constant struggle to survive. Some have long journeys. Others have short ones, but eventually everyone's journey ends. Mark's journey, cut far too short, was filled with undeniable pain and suffering, yet, was filled with amazing happiness and unconditional love. He made the best of his life by overcoming his odds with his inner strength and soft gentleness. He showed us how to love unconditionally by giving us the courage to fight the prejudices of the world. He gave our journey love, laughter, and happiness. He taught us to relish the here and now and savour the time we spend with our loved ones. He taught us a greater love and deeper grief. Our journey without Mark continues now, but with different focus. We now travel through the journey of life's unexpected turns, but Mark's journey, although it has ceased, will forever be embedded within our hearts.

SUPPORTING SIBLINGS:
A LITERATURE REVIEW WITH REFLECTIONS

Children with special needs have their own unique situations and needs. The families have to learn to deal with these situations and needs the best way they can. Unfortunately within these families there are some individuals that need special consideration, but often are forgotten. Siblings of special needs individuals play an important part in their brother or sister's development, and yet, professionals often ignore siblings. Research states that 80% of American children receiving special education services have siblings (Summers, Bridge & Summers, 1991). That is a large percentage of young individuals who need guidance and support, but aren't receiving anything. Growing up with a brother or sister with special needs can be very difficult and requires special consideration by parents and professionals. "The impact of disability on siblings may best by conceptualized as a risk or stress factor, the significance of which is mediated by other individual and family characteristics and resources" (Lobato, Faust & Spirito, 1988). Their needs are unique and vary widely from individual to individual. As a sibling of a person with multiple disabilities, I understand all too well the difficulties that can come from this special circumstance.

If all the relationships within the family are affected by the disability, it only makes sense that there would be some impact on the siblings. Three different research papers support this theory. Stoneman and Brody (1993) state that "a system approach to the study of the family rests on the assumption that families are composed of different substems that mutually influence one another." Bauer, Keefe and Shea (2001) state "the social system perspective regards each individual as developing in dynamic relationships with, and as an inseparable part of, the several social contexts or settings in which the individual either functions directly, or is affected by, throughout his or her life." Brofenbrenner's social system model (1979) explains how the different environments affect any child. The model's theory explains that every environment and person in a child's life affects him or her. From these statements one would conclude that a child with special needs would have some type of impact on their sibling. Just what kind of an impact that disability may have on a sibling can vary greatly from child to child. The reason for the variations that may affect a child comes down to the differences within each family unit. "There are a number of factors that appear to put these siblings at risk. They include parental anxieties, attitudes and expectations; family resources; sex, age and ordinal position of the non-handicapped child and the severity of the handicap." (Atkins, 1989) In order to reduce the risks to these individuals it is best that we discuss the issues they may have and how we, parents and other professionals, can best support the siblings.

The research that has been done with siblings is mixed in its findings. Even though all families are different in their characteristics, there are some similarities or themes in how a sibling of a child with a disability is affected. It was reported (Atkins, 1989) through a survey of adults with siblings with disabilities that 59% of siblings reported a negative impact, 18% reported a positive impact and 9% had no particular effect from having a sibling with a disability. Grossman (1972) found that 45% of siblings reported "that they had suffered from being a sibling of a person with mental disabilities. They reported feelings of guilt, shame, neglect, defectiveness and having negative feelings toward the brother or sister with mental disabilities." In the same study, 45% of siblings reported benefits from the experience. These included "a greater understanding of people and handicaps in particular, more compassion, more sensitive of prejudice, more appreciation of their own good health and intelligence than peers" (Grossman, 1972).

Although the research is mixed in whether or not the experience of having a sibling with a disability is positive or negative, there are definite patterns in the issues surrounding siblings. Through my review of the literature, some themes were found that could cause a negative impact on the sibling. They included increased stress and anxiety, limited attention that the sibling receives, an increased amount of care giving and household responsibilities than typical children, being teased or bullied at school, concerns for their future responsibilities, adjustment problems, and learning how to cope with complicated emotions that relate to being a sibling of a child with special needs.

There are so many issues surrounding siblings of children with disabilities that it only makes sense that they would have increased stress and anxiety from the situation. Siblings may not know what to expect from day to day. Harmer Cox, Marshall, Mandlesco and Olsen (2003) discovered "evidence that family stressors associated with raising a child with disabilities affect the day-to-day lives of siblings." They may have to deal with their sibling's illness or the possibility of death. Stoneman and Brody (1993) stated that "emotional reactions of nondisabled siblings to the ever-present possibility of crisis or death of a brother or sister with a life-threatening illness would be expected to affect the roles, warmth and closeness, and level of engagement between siblings." I constantly had nightmares that my brother was going to die. It was a very stressful situation because we never knew what was going to happen. Siblings also may not have enough information to fully understand the situation, which can lead to increased fear of the situation. Even if they have enough information, they may not fully understand the characteristics of the disability, why their sibling is disabled or if they, too, may become disabled. They may have to deal with extra responsibilities. Mandleco, Olsen, Dyches, and Marshall (2003) found that "female siblings who are older than the child with a disability reported that being responsible for the child with a disability was one of the most frequent stressors they experienced in relation to the child with a disability." In order to support siblings with their stress and anxiety, it is important for parents and professionals to empathize with the child. Try to understand where they are coming from through open communication and help them find an appropriate way to cope with their stress and anxiety.

When raising a child with a disability, there is always the concern surrounding the time spent caring for the needs of that child. Sometimes these needs are so great that the rest of the family's needs are not met. Parents spend a lot of time with the special needs child due to the extra care needed for their development. Siblings may resent the time that they miss out on with their parents. Many research studies have found that siblings of children with special needs often receive limited time and attention, which can adversely affect their life. "Siblings who are younger than the disabled child tend to suffer more than those who are older, presumable because they 'miss-out' to some extent on the exclusive care giving, usually reserved for the younger child" (Howlin, 1988). "Sibling adaptation, well-being, and coping may be affected if parents have less time and energy to meet their children's needs, limited resources for recreation and leisure and smaller social networks" (Mandleco et al., 2003). Not only do siblings receive limited attention at home, but they may be restricted in their social lives as well. Dyson (1989) found that siblings were less active in extracurricular activities and Gibbs (1993) reported that siblings were not given the same amount of time to socialize with their peers as typical children were. Parents need to be conscious of the time they spend with each child as well as how much time the sibling is spending with others outside the immediate family. Parents need to spend time alone with each child engaged in their favourite activities. Siblings need to know that they are loved just as much as the child with special needs.

Not only do siblings have to deal with limited time and attention, but they also may be expected to have more care giving and household responsibilities than other children their age. "Research has shown that older daughters who do not have a disability are typically expected to provide more care giving to a brother or sister with a disability" (Gibbs, 1993). Boyce and Barnett (1993) stated that "among families of children with retardation, there seem to be large individual differences in the amount of child care responsibilities siblings are given. When these responsibilities are great, the siblings may be negatively affected, as evidenced by increased conflict and decreased positive interaction." Turnball and Turnball (1997) and Meyer and Vadasy (1996) all stated in their research findings that siblings of children with special needs had more care giving responsibilities that may have a negative impact on their life. Parents need to be aware of the extra responsibilities that they are placing on the siblings. If it's too much for the child, find a different alternative. Respite is one great way of reducing sibling's care giving responsibilities. I did a lot of care giving for my brother while we were growing up, but my parents also used respite services so I never felt overwhelmed with the additional responsibilities.

When siblings are school-aged, they may have to face teasing or being bullied due to their special needs sibling. "Many siblings describe a friend as someone who does not make fun of a person with special needs" (Meyer and Vadasy, 1996). Unfortunately, having a sibling with a disability may cause "anger, shame, shyness or social isolation in the sibling because they or their brother/sister are teased and/or embarrassed by others" (Mandelco et al., 2003). In my experience, the word 'retard' was one that caused my heart to break. In elementary school, I was teased a great deal about my 'retarded' brother. My mom remembers me coming home in tears very frequently throughout my first few years of school. She taught me how to deal with the teasing by being a good role model and advocate for her son. It is necessary for parents to teach their child how to deal with teasing and how to stand up for their brother or sister. These skills can eventually turn into advocacy skills when they are older which can be used to help their sibling during adulthood.

This brings us to another added stressor. Siblings often are concerned for their future responsibilities. As parents age, siblings begin to realize that they may become responsible for the person with a disability. "There is evidence that many adult siblings of persons with retardation continue to be emotionally and instrumentally involved with their brother or sister throughout the lifespan" (Seltzer and Krauss, 1993). "Siblings will also worry about the impact on their own lives—on their marriage, their children, their career and their financial well-being—of assuming primary responsibility for a brother or sister with retardation" (Seltzer and Krauss, 1993). With the pressure on his or her own adult life comes the added pressure of not being prepared for the responsibility that comes with having a brother or sister with a disability. "It is likely that most siblings have an incomplete understanding of the community-based service system in their area, and may not have learned the advocacy skills that will be required of them should they assume a responsible role in the care of their family member with retardation" (Seltzer and Krauss, 1993). It is important, then, that siblings are provided with information in these areas to ease the pressure of the potential added responsibility. In my experience, I worried about whether my brother's disability was genetic and if my children would be disabled. I also remember worrying about where my brother would live or work when he got older and if it would become my responsibility to help him emotionally and financially.

With all of these issues surrounding siblings, it's not surprising that some research has found these children have difficulty adjusting to their situation, which may lead to behaviour problems. Gibbs (1993), as found by Lobato (1990), stated that "oldest daughters (especially in low SES families) have consistently been found to have the greatest likelihood of adjustment difficulties." Faux (1993), as reported by Mandleco et al. (2003) found that "siblings who were older than the child with disabilities displayed more problem behaviours." Harmer Cox et al. (2003) identified "difficulty in school setting, jealousy, decreased self-esteem and social isolation" as some of the behaviour problems that siblings may experience. However, on the opposite end of the spectrum, many studies have found these individuals to be well adjusted. Dyson (1989) stated that siblings "displayed the same level of self-concept, behaviour problems and social competence as matched siblings of non-handicapped children" and that "brothers of handicapped children were less aggressive and hyperactive and tended to have fewer externalizing behaviour problems than brothers of non-handicapped children." In the NICHY News Digest (Valdiviesco, Ripley & Ambler, 1988), it was stated that "children with disabled siblings appear to have more positive and fewer negative behavioural interactions than do those with nondisabled siblings." Lobato, Faust and Spirito (1988) found "many siblings of disabled children appear to benefit emotionally and psychologically from the experience." It appears then that the experience of having a sibling with a disability can have different effects on a child's behaviour. From the different findings within the research, behaviour problems may be caused by risk factors related to the family situation or the child's personality and not just the disability itself.

Siblings experience a variety of complicated emotions during the course of their life. Singer and Powers (1993) and Meyer and Vadasy (1996) both explained that guilt was often an emotion these children have to deal with. They may think they caused the disability their sibling has or they may feel guilty for not having the disability themselves. I remember feeling very guilty because I thought I had caused my brother's disability. Of course I didn't, but young children do not fully understand the cause behind the disability. Younger siblings may "feel guilty for developing skills that their older sibling with disabilities have not yet mastered" (Gibbs, 1993). They "may experience jealousy and feelings of anger toward their brother or sister with a disability, which in turn may cause them to feel guilty" (Opperman & Alant, 2003). These individuals may also wonder if their sibling's disability is contagious. "Siblings with mild disabilities may be more likely to identify with the sibling and perhaps fear they too may have or acquire a disability" (Gibbs, 1993). Meyer and Vadasy (1996) also stated that loneliness could become an issue for these individuals. They may feel they have no one to turn to because no one understands what it's like to have a sibling with a disability. As a teenager, I remember thinking that there was nobody else who knew what I was going through. It wasn't until my university days that I realized I wasn't alone. Siblings may feel resentment toward their parents for the lack of attention or they may copy their sibling's negative behaviour to seek attention. They may be angry about the situation that they are in and not know how to handle this anger appropriately. They also may feel more pressure to succeed to make up for their sibling's disability. "The sibling may feel that he or she has a responsibility to attempt to alleviate it by being 'extra-good'" (Powell and Gallagher, 1993). Because of these complicated emotions, it's important that parents allow siblings to express themselves. There needs to be open communication within the family so that the child learns its okay to feel a certain way and that everyone can work together to make the emotions more positive.

Regardless of all the negative issues surrounding siblings, research has found that they can and do benefit from the experience. Lobato (1990) and Powell and Gallagher (1993) all found that siblings could become "more mature, more responsible, self-confident, independent and patient. These siblings can also become more altruistic (charitable), more sensitive to humanitarian efforts, and have a greater sense of closeness." Gibbs (1993) stated that "growing up with a difference in the family can offer the child a unique opportunity to confront society's discriminations and gain perspective on the deeper meaning of life." The interaction between a child with a disability and his/her sibling is quite different than that of a typical sibling. Gibbs (1993) also described the interactions as more "instrumental/teaching types of behaviours." Stoneman and Brody (1993) found that "many siblings seemed to be quite adept at selecting play materials and activities that could bridge the competency differences between themselves and their siblings with mental retardation." Often times it seems these children pick up ways of interacting with their sibling through therapy sessions or parent modelling (Gibbs, 1993). These are valuable skills that siblings can transfer into a future career. This is maybe a reason why Simeonsson and McHale (1981), as reported in Singers and Powers (1993), found that "older sisters of children with disabilities are more likely to pursue careers in the helping professions." Atkins (1987) found that siblings are "less likely to judge on the basis of appearance." Meyer and Vadasy (1996) found that siblings had "enhanced maturity, self-concept, social competence, insight, tolerance, pride, vocational opportunities, advocacy and loyalty." Harmer Cox et al. (2003) found "siblings more protective and caring of the impaired child and demonstrated increased empathy for others and less self-centeredness." In my experience I felt that I learned many lessons from my brother.

He showed me the differences in people that can sometimes stop others from seeing the natural beauty within the person. He taught me to look beyond face value and dive deeper into my soul. He allowed me to see the miracle of life even with its unhappiness. The most important thing he taught me was how to love unconditionally.

To make sure that siblings benefit from the experience as well as help them learn how to cope with the complicated issues that surround them, they need support from parents, professionals and other siblings. Accurate information and plenty of support from parents and professionals is needed. "A lack of information or misinformation about a handicapping condition can lead to unwarranted worries or fears" (Powell and Gallagher, 1993). Parents and professionals can provide these individuals with age-appropriate information throughout the siblings' lives. "Many siblings express being distressed by a lack of information or understanding of the handicapping condition" (Atkins, 1989). Information surrounding the child's disability, how to cope with the emotions they may have, how to communicate these emotions appropriately rather than acting out, how to interact appropriately with their sibling, how to deal with teasing, knowledge of future responsibilities and adult supports for people with disabilities are all examples of information that siblings will need at different stages of their lives.

Parents are the biggest support that siblings receive throughout their lives, but it is important for parents to know how best to support their children. "One of the most powerful influences on sibling adjustment appears to be the ability of parents to convey positive attitudes about the impaired child" (Grossman, 1972). The way the parent accepts the child's disability gives the sibling a role model of how they should deal with the situation. Siblings watch their parents for guidance in knowing how to deal with their special circumstances. Siblings seem to do best when parents and other adults in their lives can accept their brother or sister's disability and clearly value them as an individual. Among the other suggestions provided throughout this paper as well as the tips section included at the end, it appears that a parent's attitude and acceptance is key to the adjustment of the sibling.

Professionals such as teachers, therapists, or agency support personal can help siblings in a variety of other ways. Gibbs (1993) stated that professionals can "assist families in recognizing the needs of siblings and encourage open communication," "make information and resources available to families" and "can include siblings in early intervention programs." Professionals can provide parents with resources like books, videos, magazines and Internet sites to help siblings. Professionals can also just be there to listen. Families, and especially siblings, often just need someone to talk to that wouldn't judge what they say.

Besides the support siblings can receive from parents and professionals, other siblings can be a valuable resource. Sibling groups can provide a sibling a place to learn information about the disability, understand and cope with their feelings and learn how to problem solve for their tough situations. Powell and Gallagher (1993) state that self-help support groups are one of the most popular forms of building social support for families with children who have exceptionalities. "Listening to the experiences of other brothers and sisters in similar situations can help siblings deal with their frustrations" (Atkins, 1987). Just meeting other siblings can help eliminate the isolation these children often feel. With the technology that is out there today, meeting another sibling is just seconds away with the different web sites that can connect siblings with other siblings. I wish I'd had that support available for me when I was growing up, as I may not have felt as isolated as I did.

I feel very fortunate to have had wonderful parents who supported me and provided me with as many resources as they could. One of my brother's teachers also provided me with support especially when I was attending university. At university I met other siblings who have helped me realize that I'm not alone in this experience. These support systems helped me become the special education teacher that I am today. Because not all siblings have these supports, I feel a responsibility to bring awareness to sibling issues. We, as professionals, parents, and other siblings have a responsibility to support siblings of children with disabilities in the best possible way. Without our support, they may grow up without benefiting from the experience of growing up with a disabled sibling. It can be a very beneficial and rewarding experience, so we need to help these children learn the great life lessons that only those with disabilities can teach us.

TIPS FOR PARENTS

Provide siblings with age-appropriate material.
- Find books, videos, magazines and Internet sites for siblings.
- Realize that the need for information is a life-long process. Siblings will need information at different stages of their life.

Provide siblings with the opportunity to meet other siblings.
- Take your child to sibling support groups if they are offered in your community.
- Take your child to Special Olympics to let them help out.
- Find another family that has a child with special needs and spend time with them as a family.

Set aside time for each sibling.
- Schedule special time with each sibling doing things they enjoy.
- Attend your child's activities as often as possible. They need your support just as much as the child with special needs.

Communication is key.
- Allow and encourage your children to express their feelings, both positive and negative. They need to know that they can express their emotions without getting in trouble.
- Ask your children how they are feeling about the situation.
- Explain the disability to your child in terms they can understand.
- Ask them how you can help them deal with their sibling's disability.
- Really listen and try to understand what they are saying.
- Involve everyone in family decisions.
- Be open and honest about what is going on, especially during times of stress (illness, hospital stays, transition times, new experiences, etc.).
- Praise and discipline all your children.

Plan for the future of the child with special needs.
- Share your plans with the sibling so they don't worry about what their responsibilities might be.
- Don't expect the child to want to take responsibility for their sibling as they get older. They may not want to.
- If they want some responsibility, let the sibling help with some of the decisions.

Let kids be kids.
- Let siblings settle their own differences if they can.
- They need chances to act like "normal" siblings. They will fight, get angry at each other, and say hurtful things. Realize that this is normal.
- Welcome other children into your home to give all your children fun time.
- Don't expect the sibling to want to let the child with special needs spend time with their friends. Let the sibling decide when the child can spend time with them and when they can't.

Use services that you are entitled to.
- Limit the care giving responsibilities for the sibling. That is your responsibility, not your child's. Use the respite services that you are entitled to.
- Use respite time for individual breaks, time spent with each child, time spent together as a couple. Don't feel guilty about it. You need a break, too.
- Use any other services that are available to you.
- Join a family support group and encourage the siblings to join a sibling support group.

Allow the sibling to be involved as much or as less as they want.
- Take the child to IEP/IFSP/ITP meetings if they want to.
- Allow them to be involved in family decisions.

- Tell them where all your important files are in case of an emergency.
- Encourage your children to provide suggestions in different situations.

Treat each of your children as a special person.
- Recognize each child's strengths, qualities and the contribution they make to the family.
- Encourage each child's interests and allow them to have their own life.
- Celebrate each child's accomplishments.

Try to read your child's cues.
- Each child will have different cues when they need help with a situation, or when they need extra attention.
- Recognize times that are more stressful to siblings and try to plan for these situations to make them more positive experiences.

Keep expectations of all children within their ability.
- Chores should be at each child's ability level. Most children can do something to help out at home.
- Don't put too much pressure on the "normal" child. They may always try to be the "perfect" child to help the parents out, but this is not healthy.
- Siblings may try or be expected to be "little helpers," but you need to take extra care to not go overboard. Siblings can help out, but should not be expected to all the time.

You are only human.
- We all make mistakes and parents are no different. Forgive yourself for the mistakes you've made and try to learn from them.
- Recognize when you need a break and take it!
- Find close friends to give you the support you need.

Take care of yourself.
- You can only take care of your family when you take care of yourself.
- Spend some good quality time with yourself. It will help keep things in perspective.

Learn all you can.
- Go to conferences and workshops.
- Read books, brochures, and magazines.
- Search the Internet, but make sure what you've read is from a reliable source.
- Go to support groups for extra support and information.
- Talk to your child's teacher. They can provide you with information as well.

Make suggestions at "teachable moments."
- When things happen, be a role model and show them how they should respond.
- When things are going bad, teach your child to problem solve.
- Recognize that you are the most important teacher of your children. How your children deal with things will depend on how you deal with things.
- Help the child accept the disability by showing your acceptance of the disability.

Teach siblings the difference between supporting their brother/sister and doing things for themselves.
- Teach the child how to interact with their sibling and how to make the most of those times.
- Siblings can be advocates at home, school, on the playground and in the community. Give your child the tools to be that person.
- Teach the child with special needs to be as independent as possible. This will be your biggest gift to them and your family!

TIPS FOR PROFESSIONALS

Treat the Sibling as an Individual.
- Recognize their personality, strengths, and achievements.
- Have conversations with them that revolve around their life, not their sibling's life.
- Recognize when they want to talk and when they don't want to talk about their sibling.
- Don't compare the sibling with the child with special needs. Each person is an individual.

Be available to talk to the sibling.
- Listen to their problems or concerns.
- Give them advice on what you can.
- Find more resources on things you don't know about.
- Listen to their point of view and try to empathize with them.
- Find someone else with more experience to talk to the sibling. A great example would be another sibling.

Talk with the parents.
- Provide the parents with resources for all their children, not just the special needs child.
- Help the parents understand the unique needs of all their children.
- Keep the lines of communication open.
- Listen to what the parents have to say. They know their children better than you do, but they also may miss certain things because their lives are so busy.

Help the sibling understand Special Education.
- Take them on tours of their sibling's classrooms.
- Discuss their sibling's daily school experience.
- Set up a meeting between the special education teacher and the sibling for them to discuss the different aspects of special education.

Provide educational experiences for the sibling.
- Have the sibling do a project on their sibling's disability and present it to the class if the child wants to.
- In daily classroom activities, provide teaching experiences to teach compassion for people with differences.
- Provide teaching opportunities to learn about all different types of disabilities and make all students more aware of the special situations.
- A regular teacher should consult with the special education teacher for resources and support.

Provide the sibling with age-appropriate information.
- Siblings have a life long need for information.
- At each stage of a sibling's life, they need different kinds of information.
- Only give them the information they can handle, but realize that they can handle more than you think.

Parents are trying their best.
- Do not judge the parents. Each situation is different and they are doing the best with what they have.
- Recognize that their values in life are different than yours and that you might not always see eye to eye.
- Realize that their life is full of many stressors.
- They have good days and bad days just like you.

TIPS FOR SIBLINGS

Love your sibling.
- Realize that it is a sibling relationship. You will fight. You will get mad at each other. You will have ups and downs, but you will forever be siblings.

Communicate your feelings.
- Express yourself, but don't beat yourself up over your feelings. You have a right to feel the way you do.
- Let your parents know when you need extra attention.
- Talk to your parents about your feelings (e.g. guilt, loneliness, and sadness).
- Tell your parents when you are being bullied about having a sibling with a disability.

Learn all you can.
- At each stage in your life, you will need different types of information because you will have different questions and concerns.
- Find out about your sibling's disability.
- Find out about your sibling's education.
- Find out about your sibling's life and future.

Talk to another sibling.
- Nobody knows better what it's like to have a sibling with a disability than another sibling.
- Share your feelings and concerns with them. They can help.
- It would be especially helpful to find an older sibling, because they could share how they dealt with it and provide information that you will need to know in the future.

Be involved in a sibling support group if one is offered in your community.
- Sibshops can provide you with opportunities for information and support that no one else can provide you.

Learn how to be an advocate for your sibling.
- Growing up with a sibling with special needs, may require you to protect your sibling by sticking up for them.
- Learn how to stop bullying.
- Learn how to help people understand your sibling.
- Realize that as your sibling grows up you may need to take a greater role in their life.
- Learn what you can and learn how to stand up for your sibling.

You have a right to your own life.
- Don't feel guilty about having your own friends, your own interests and your own achievements.
- Your life deserves to be celebrated as well!
- You have your own personality, with your own strengths and weaknesses.
- Remember that you are an individual and you have different needs than your sibling.

Talk to your parents about your concerns for the future.
- Encourage your parents to make plans for your sibling's future.
- Encourage your parents to include you in these plans so you know what to expect.
- If you are not willing to be responsible for your sibling in the future, be sure you tell your parents. You don't have to do anything you don't want to do.

Make a list of the benefits you've gained from being a sibling.
- Do a list of pros and cons of having a sibling with a disability.
- You have learned many life lessons that many people never learn in their entire lives!

RESOURCES FOR PARENTS, SIBLINGS AND PROFESSIONALS

* There are lists and lists of children and adult books on people with special needs. Type books and disabilities in to any search engine and it will bring you to these lists.

BOOKS FOR PARENTS/ADULT SIBLINGS:

Berg, S., Kinsey, D., Lutke, J. & Whiway, D. (1997). *A layman's guide to FAS and possible FAE.* FAS/E Support Network of BC.

Carter, J. (2000). *To love this life: Quotations by Helen Keller.* American Foundation for the Blind and Scholastic, Inc.

Dash, J. (2001). *The world at her fingertips: The story of Helen Keller.* Scholastic, Inc.

Facing the Crowd: Managing other people's insensitivities to your child. (1987). Shannon Books.

Harris, S.L. (1994). *Siblings of children with autism: A guide for families.* Woodbine House.

Groom, W. (1986). *Forrest gump.* New York: Simon and Schuster, Inc.

Klein, S.D. & Schleifer, M.J. (1993). *It isn't fair! Siblings of Children with disabilities.* Bergin & Garvey.

Lavin, J.L. (2001). *Special kids need special parents: A resource for parents of children with special needs.* Berkley Trade Publishing.

Lobato, D.J. (1990). *Brothers, Sisters and Special Needs: Information and activities for helping young siblings of children with illnesses and developmental disabilities.* Baltimore, Maryland: Paul H. Brookes Publishing Company.

Manitoba Education and Training. (2004). *Working together: A handbook for parents of children with special needs.*

Massimilla, E. (1956). *Heaven's Very Special Child.* Hatboro, PA: This is Our Life Publishing. This Is Our Life Publications, Box 21, Hatboro, PA 19040 USA

Maurice, C. (1993). *Let me hear your voice: A family triumphs over autism.* New York: Random House.

McCaffrey, F.D. & Fish, T. (1989). *Profiles of the other child: A sibling guide for Parents.* Ohio State University Nisonger Center.

McCluskey, K. (1996). *Butterfly kisses: Amber's journey through hyperactivity.* Queenston, ON: Marvin Melnyk Associates.

McHugh, M. (1999). *Special siblings growing up with someone with a disability.*

Meyer, D., Vadasy, P. & Pillo, C. (1995). *Sibshops: Workshops for siblings of children with special needs.* Baltimore, Maryland: Paul H. Brookes Publishing Company

Meyer, D. *Uncommon fathers: Reflections on raising a child with a disability.*

Moorman, M. (1992). *My sister's keeper: Learning to cope with a sibling's mental illness.* W.W. Norton and Company, Inc.

Powell, T.H. & Gallagher, P.A. *Brothers and sisters: A special part of exceptional families.* (1993). Baltimore, Maryland: Paul H. Brookes Publishing Company.

Sullivan, G. (2000). *In their own words: Helen Keller.* Scholastic, Inc.

BOOKS FOR SIBLINGS:

Anderson, K. (1982). *Don't forget me, mommy!* Marin Publishing Co.

Baker, P. J. (1986). *My first book of sign.* Washington, DC: Kendall Green Publications.

Blackburn, L.B. (1991). *I know I made it happen: A gentle book about feeling guilty.* Centering Corp.

Bleach, F. *Everybody is different: A book for young people who have brothers or sisters with autism.*

Byars, B. (1996). *The Summer of the swans.* Scholastic, Inc.

Cairo, S. (1988). *Our brother has down's syndrome.*

Children's Television Workshop. (1980). *Sign language fun with Linda Bove.* Muppets, Inc.

Dodds, B. *My sister annie.*

Edwards, B. (1999). *My brother, sammy.* Mulbrook Pr. Trade

Emmett, M. (1989). *I'm the big sister now.* Albert Whitman.

Fain, K. (1993). *Handsigns: A sign language alphabet.* Scholastic, Inc.

Gifaldi, D. *Ben, king of the river.*

Kates, B.J. (1992). *We're different, we're the same featuring Jim Henson's sesame street muppets.* New York: Random House.

Meyer, D. (1997). *Views from our shoes: Growing up with a brother or sister with special needs.* Woodbine House Publishing.

Meyer, D. & Vadasy, P. (1996). *Living with a brother or sister with special needs.* Washington Press. (has an excellent list of children's books for all ages).

Pulver, R. (1999). *Way to go, Alex!*

Rosenberg, M.B. (1998). *Finding a way: Living with exceptional brothers and sisters.* Lothrop, Lee and Shepherd books.

Seigel, B. & Silverstein, S. (1994). *What about me? Growing up with a developmentally disabled sibling.* Penum Press.

Simon, R. (2002). *Riding the bus with my sister: A true life journey.*

Shriver, M. (2001). *What's wrong with Timmy.* Little, Brown and Company Inc. and Warner Books, Inc.

Shyer, M.F. (1988). *Welcome home, jellybean.*

Stuve-Bodeen, S. (1998). *We'll Paint the Octopus Red.*

Tashjian, J. (1997). *Tru confessions.*

Thompson, M. (1992). *My brother Matthew.*

BOOKS FOR TEACHERS:

Berg, S., Kinsey, D, Lutke, J. & Whiway, D. (1997). *A layman's guide to FAS and possible FAE.* FAS/E Support Network of BC.

Berg, S., Kinsey, D, Lutke, J. & Whiway, D. (1997). *FAS/E and education: The art of making a difference.* FAS/E Support Network of BC.

Collins, S. (1992). *Signing at school.* Eugene, OR: Garlic Press.

Kitterman, J. & Collins, S.H. (1991). *A word in the hand: An introduction to sign Language. Books 1 & 2.* Eugene, OR: Stanley Collins.

Manitoba Education and Training. (1998). *Individual education planning: A handbook for developing and implementing IEP's, Early to Senior Years.*

Manitoba Education and Training. (2001). *Special needs categorical funding process update.*

Manitoba Education and Training. (2001). *Towards inclusions: from challenges to possibilities: planning for behaviour.*

Meyer, D., Vadasy, P. & Pillo, C. (1995). *Sibshops: Workshops for siblings of children with special needs.* Baltimore, Maryland: Paul H. Brookes Publishing Company.

Singer, G.H.S. & Powers, L.E. (1993). *Families, disabilities and empowerment: Active coping skills and strategies for family interventions.* Baltimore, Maryland: Paul H. Brookes Publishing Company.

Society for Manitobans with Disabilities. (2002). *SMD and ME*.

Turnball, A.P. & Turnball, H.R. (1997). *Families, professionals, and exceptionality: A special partnerships*. Prentice-Hall, Inc.

Warren, J. & Shroyer, S. (1992). *Piggyback songs to sign*. Warren Publishing House.

INTERNET SITES:

Council for Exceptional Children.
www.cec.sped.org

Learning Disabilities Resources.
www.teachersfirst.com/learn-dis.htm

Meyer, D. *The Sibling Support Project.*
www.thearc.org/siblingsupport

A Sibling's Site.
www.asiblingssite.com

Siblings: Brothers and sisters of people who have Mental Retardation.
www.thearc.org/faqs/siblings.html

Siblings of Disabled Kids and Peers offering Promise.
www.SodaPopOnline.org

Special Education Free Worksheets.
www.specialed.freeyellow.com

Special Education Links.
www.halcyon.com/marcs/sped.html

Special Sibling Relief.
www.specialsiblingrelief.4mg.com

Special Needs Education - Canada's School Net.
www.schoolnet.sne

Teaching Ideas for Early Childhood Special Education.
www.mcps.k12.md.us/curriculum/pep/teach.htm

VIDEOS/MOVIES:

Benny and Joon. (1993). Starring Johnny Depp, Mary Stuart Masterson and Aidan Quinn. A story of a mentally ill young woman who finds love.

Disney's The Hunchback of Notre Dame. (1996). Animated: Through the story of a deformed man who stands up for himself and his friend, children learn that differences are okay.

Dominick and Eugene. (1988). Starring Ray Liotta, Tom Hulce and Jamie Lee Curtis. The story of twins (one who is intellectually challenged while the other studies to become a doctor) as they struggle to figure out their lives.

Forrest Gump. (1994). Starring Tom Hanks. A story about a mentally challenged man who witnesses many historical moments while being in love with a troubled woman.

I Am Sam. (2001). Starring Sean Penn. A mentally challenged man fights for custody of his daughter.

The Miracle Worker. (2000). TV version starring Hallie Kate Eisnberg. The story of Helen Keller and her teacher, Annie Sullivan.

The Miracle Worker. (1962). Starring Anne Bancroft and Patty Duke. The story of Helen Keller and her teacher, Annie Sullivan.

Molly. (1999). Starring Elizabeth Shue and Aaron Eckhart. A mentally challenged woman moves in with her brother, undergoes experimental treatments and causes disruptions in her brother's life.

Mr. Holland's Opus. (1995). Starring Richard Dryfuss. A high school music teacher and composer must deal with his deaf son.

The Other Sister. (1999). Starring Juliette Lewis and Diane Keaton. A mentally challenged young woman moves back home and make her family realize she's grown up and falling in love.

Rain Man. (1988). Starring Tom Cruise and Dustin Hoffman. A story about a man who discovers his father gave his inheritance to an autistic brother that he never knew existed.

"We're the Sibs." Markfield Project, Markfield Road. London N15 4RB

What's Eating Gilbert Grape? (1993). Starring Leonardo DiCaprio and Johnny Depp. A young man cares for his autistic brother and obese mother which cause problems in his life.

SPECIAL EDUCATION GLOSSARY

AAC - augmentative and alternative communication; different ways to communicate with other people (i.e. communication devices, communication boards, etc.)

Accessible - buildings that have a way for a person with a disability to enter the building or have special designs on the inside to help people with disabilities (i.e. ramps, handicapped washrooms, automatic doors, railings, elevators, etc.)

ACL - Association for Community Living; an organization dedicated to making the lives of adults with disabilities more rewarding

Adaptive Equipment - any special equipment used to help a person with disabilities with a particular skill (e.g. wheelchairs, standing frames, walkers, etc)

Advocate - a person representing others in an effort to bring change that will eliminate barriers for special needs.

AFO - ankle foot orthoses; braces on the foot to help position the foot

Age-Appropriate - activities for students with disabilities that are similar to what their peers would be doing

Assessment - different tools (checklists, tests, standardized tests, observations, rubrics, etc.) used to collect information for the purpose of evaluating students' skills

At-risk children - children who are in danger of developing a disability due to events that happen prior to, during, or directly after birth; children can also be at risk for developing a disability due to environmental issues during their first few years of life if early intervention services are not provided

Backward Chaining - a teaching tool, you start with the last step of the task and link each tiny step together until the entire task is mastered

Behaviour Modification - technique of shaping behaviour by reinforcing desirable responses and ignoring undesirable responses

Bill 17 - *The Public School Amendment Act,* introduced by the Manitoba Government in April 2003. This amendment to *The Public Schools Act* will ensure that all students in Manitoba are entitled to receive appropriate educational programming that fosters students' participation in both the academic and social life of the school. The legislation will assist all students, particularly those with special needs, in receiving the appropriate educational services they require." Author Note: this law was just coming into effect when the book was being published. For more information see the Manitoba Education and Training Website

CFS - Child and Family Services; an organization that provides services and supports to children with special needs and their families

Chronological Age - the number of years and months since birth

Circle of Friends - a program designed for students with disabilities to help them develop close friendships

Communication Boards - involve picture symbols that people with disabilities point at to tell someone what they want (see chapter 13 for more information)

Communication Devices - different technology that people with disabilities use to communicate with others (e.g. Dynamyte, Dynavox)

Communication Domain – how a person interacts with others (i.e. speech, non-verbal (gestures), communication devices/boards, sign language)

Communication Log - a notebook/organizer sent back and forth between school and home for students who have difficulty communicating; teachers and parents share events of the day/night with each other

CSW - community service worker who helps provide services and supports for people with disabilities

Data - written record of different information (i.e. written notes about a behaviour)

Day Services - a program where the adult with disability is assisted in finding and maintaining a job, providing on-site support and job training, job-related skills; can be done in the community setting or at a day service facility

Developmentally Delayed - students/children who are not developing at the same level as their age peers

Disability - a person who has a weakness or is unable to do something in a particular area

Early Intervention - any service provided to children age birth to 5 to assist them in developing skills

EMH - educable mentally handicapped; a student that is diagnosed as EMH can benefit from an academic based curriculum

FAPE - free appropriate public education; students with disabilities are guaranteed the right to an education; this is used in PL 94-142 in the US

Forward Chaining - a teaching technique, you start with the first step of the task and link each tiny step together until the entire task is mastered

Functional Academics - "real-life" academic skills that are needed to become independent in today's society (i.e. writing a letter, reading a newspaper, filling in forms, counting money, etc.)

Funding - money paid by the government to help children with special needs receive services they need (in a school setting there are three levels of funding, Level 1, Level 2 and Level 3 (most amount of funding); which level the students are at depends on the severity of the child's disability; school receives more money for different kids)

Gesture prompt - a teacher gives a student direction on a task by using a pre-taught hand motion

Group Home - a home designed for people with disabilities where they can receive 24-hour care

Hand-over-hand - when a child is learning an activity, a teacher places their hand directly over the student's hand to help them complete the activity

Home School - school child would attend if they didn't have a disability

IEP - Individualized Education Plan; a plan written for students aged 5-14; a written plan developed by a team (parents, teachers, therapists, etc.) stating outcomes and objectives that the child needs to work on; also states child's background information, current level of ability in all areas, method, materials and strategies to help achieve specific skills, names of members and plans to evaluate student's progress

IEP meeting - a meeting for a child's team, composed of teachers, parents, therapists, etc., to discuss the child's IEP

IFSP - individualized family service plan; a plan created for a child with special needs aged birth to 5 and their family, the plan explains the needed services and goals for the family

Inclusion - including people with disabilities within the school setting; inclusion can look very different for each child; According to Manitoba, Education and Youth (2000), inclusion is a way of thinking and acting that allows each individual to feel accepted, valued, and safe.

Income Assistance - individuals with disabilities receive financial assistance from the government depending on how much they make at their job; the money helps them make ends meet, individuals also receive a variety of benefits such as medical and dental on this program.

Independent Living Domain - skills a person needs to live by themselves (cooking, cleaning, money management, etc.)

IPP - individualized program plan; can be used to refer to any of the plans (IFSP, IEP, ITP); also a written plan for an adult with a disability that states the goals that person will strive for during a year and how they can be achieved

IQ - intelligence quotient; how a child relates to others in the same age group; below 70 on an intelligence test (Stanford-Binet or the Wechsler Scales) is considered in the mentally disabled range

ITP - Individualized Transition Plan; for children aged 14 and older; it is a written plan that focuses on their future living arrangements and vocational abilities that are needed for the child's independence

Life Skills - any skill that a student would need to learn to become independent in "real-life"

MAPS - McGill Action Planning System; a meeting used to help plan a student's education plan (see chapter 12 for more information)

Mental Age - where a child is mentally developing; intellectual level

Mental Retardation - Mental retardation refers to substantial limitations in present functioning. It is characterized by significantly subaverage intellectual functioning, existing concurrently with related limitations in two or more of the following applicable adaptive skill areas: communication, self-care, home living, social skills, community use, self-direction, health and safety, functional academics, leisure and work. Mental retardation manifests before age 18. (DSM-IV definition)

Microcephaly - abnormal smallness of the head resulting in a mental disability

Moderate Disability - a disability that requires lots of assistance

Multiple Disabilities - a person would have more than one disability

Occupational Therapist - someone who helps a person strengthen fine (little) motor muscles

Orthotic Devices - any device used to brace a limb or spine to help in gross or fine motor activities

Parent Support Group - a group for parents of children with disabilities aimed at providing information and support

Parking Permit Program - Bill 47 of the Manitoba Highway Traffic Act; states that it is illegal to park in reserved handicapped parking unless the vehicle has a permit

PATH - Planning Alternative Tomorrows with Hope; a planning tool to help adults with disabilities plan their future (see chapter 19 for more information)

PL 94-142 - Education for all Handicapped Children Act; passed in 1975 in the United States, it guarantees students with disabilities a right to an education

Physical Prompt - teacher moves the student's body to give directions to complete a task

Physiotherapist - someone who helps a child strengthen gross (big) motor muscles

Receptive Language - the message a child receives from other people

Residential Home - a home designed for people with disabilities where they can receive 24-hour care

Respite – when a child with a disability spends time with someone outside the family so that the family can have a break

Respite Worker - someone who is paid by the government to look after a child with a disability while the parents/family take a needed break

Resource Room - a classroom within a school where children can receive one-on-one assistance in their schoolwork

SDM - substitute decision maker; refers to a person who can make decisions for a person with a disability under the Vulnerable Person's Act

SERI - Special Education Review Initiative; a process used to evaluate and improve special education in Manitoba

Self-Care - skills needed to take care of your personal grooming (i.e. grooming, getting dressed, etc.)

Severe Disabilities - functioning at a level between moderate and profoundly disabled; person often has more than one disability and needs lots of care

Sibling Support Groups - a group for siblings of children with disabilities aimed at providing information and support

SIBS - a child with a brother or sister who has a disability

Sibshops - another name for a sibling support group

SMH - severe mental handicap; a severe disability that requires lots of assistance for the rest of that person's life

Social Skills Domain - how to get along with other people; people with mental disabilities often have difficulty with these skills and need to be taught

Special Education - any education that is different from what a regular child would receive

Special Needs - a person who has different needs from other people; in education this term is used for those who have academic difficulties

Special Services Classrooms - students remain in this classroom for most of the school day and receive training in specific skills needed for their independence

Speech Pathologist - someone who teaches a child to communicate by either using speech, gestures, sign language, or machines

Stanford-Binet Intelligence Scales - an intelligence test given by a trained psychologist; from this test a person would receive an IQ score

Standing Frame - a piece of specialized adaptive equipment; helps a child build the muscles and posture needed to stand

Summer programs - programs set up for students with disabilities during the summer months to help the students keep their skills

Supported Living - a program to assist individuals with disabilities in their living arrangements; can be done either at home, their own home, or a group/residential facility

Task Analysis - a task that is broken down into tiny steps; a teaching tool

Therapy Putty - like Play-doh except more strong; used to strength fine motor skills in students with disabilities

TMH - trainable mental handicap; a moderate disability requiring assistance from others; school emphasize is on training of basic functional skills

Transition - moving from one area of life to the next; it is important to plan for each transition in the life of a child with a disability

Verbal Prompt - what a teacher gives a student to help learn a task (i.e., encouragement, directions to a step, helpful hint, etc.)

Vocational Domain - job-related skills that people need to get and maintain a job

Vocational Rehabilitation - provides services to help individual obtain and maintain employment

Vulnerable Person's Act - an act designed to protect the rights of people with mental disabilities who need assistance to meet their needs; called the Vulnerable Person's Living with a Mental Disability Act

Wechsler Intelligence Scales - an intelligence test given by a trained psychologist; a person receives an IQ score from this test

REFERENCES

American Psychiatric Association. (1994). *Diagnostic and Statistical Manual of Mental Disorders (4th edition)*. Washington, D.C.

Atkins, D.V. (1987). Siblings of the hearing impaired: perspectives for parents. *Volta Review*, 89(5), 32-45.

Atkins, S.P. (1989). Siblings of handicapped children. *Child and adolescent social work*, 6(4), 271-282.

Bauer, A.M., Keefe, C.H., Shea, T.M. (2001). *Students with Learning disabilities or emotional/behavioural disorders*. Upper Saddle Rover, NJ: Prentice-Hall, Inc.

Beirne-Smith, M., Patton, J.R., & Ittenback, R. (1994). *Mental retardation* (4th ed.). Englewood Cliffs, New Jersey: Macmillan Publishing Company.

Berkobren, R. (n.d.) *Down Syndrome: Siblings: Brothers and Sisters who have Mental Retardation*. Retrieved February 24, 2004, from http://www.nas.com/downsyn/sibling.htm

Boyce, G.C. & Barnett, W.S. (1993). Siblings of persons with mental retardation: A historical perspective and recent findings. In Z. Stoneman & P.W. Berman (Eds), *The effects of mental retardation, disability and illness on sibling relationships*, (pp.145-181). Baltimore, Maryland: Paul H. Brookes Publishing Company.

Boychuk, J. (Personal communications about income tax deductions for people with disabilities, June 2004).

Brandon University. (1998-2004). Kimberley Smith's Graduate classes notes.

Brofenbrenner, U. (1979). *The ecology of human development.* Cambridge, MA: Harvard University Press.

Canada Customs and Revenue Agency: Disability Tax Credit. (2004) Retrieved June 28, 2004 from, www.cra-arc.gc.ca

Children's Special Services. (2002). *Children's Special Services Information on Programs.* Retrieved June 2002 from: www.gov.mb.ca/fs/programs

Contact a Family for Families with Disabled Children: Sibling fact sheet. (2003). Retrieved February 24, 2004, from: http://www.cafamily.org.uk/siblings.html

Dyson, L. (1989). Adjustment of siblings of handicapped children: A comparison. *Journal of pediatric psychology,* 14(2), 215-229.

Dyson, L., Edgar, E. & Crnic, K. (1989). Psychological predictors of adjustment by siblings of developmentally disabled children. *American Journal on Mental Retardation,* 94, 292-302.

Eric Clearinghouse on Disabilities and Gifted Education: Siblings of Children with Disabilities. (2002). Retrieved February 25, 2004, from http://ericec.org/faq/siblings.html

Faux, S.A. (1993). Siblings of children with chronic physical and cognitive disabilities. *Journal of Pediatric Nursing,* 8(5), 305-317.

Ferguson, B. (1994). *Mark Leslie's Funeral Service.*

Focus: Brothers and Sisters. (1997). *Disability Solutions,* 2(3), Sept/Oct.

Gibbs, B. (1993). Providing support to sisters and brothers of children with disabilities. In G. Singers & L. Powers (Eds.) *Families, disability and empowerment: Active coping skills and strategies for family interventions.* Baltimore, Maryland: Paul H. Brookes Publishing Company.

Grossman, F. (1972). *Brothers and sisters of retarded children.* Syracuse University Press, Syracuse.

Harmer Cox, A., Marshall, E.S., Mandlesco, B. & Olsen, S.F. (2003). Coping responses to daily life stressors of children who have a sibling with a disability. *Journal of Family Nursing*, 9(4), 397-413.

Howlin, P. (1988). Living with impairment: the effects on children of having an autistic sibling. *Child: care, health & development,* 14, 395-408.

Kingsley, E.P. (1987). *Welcome to Holland.*

LeClere, F.B. & Kowalewski, B.M. (1994). Disability in the family: The effects on children's well-being. *Journal of Marriage and the family*, 56 (2), 457-468.

Leslie, D., Leslie, J. & Leslie, T. (Personal communications throughout life as well as Mark's files).

Lobato, D.J. (1990). *Brothers, sisters and special needs: Information and activities for helping young siblings with chronic illnesses and developmental disabilities.* Baltimore, Maryland: Paul H. Brookes Publishing Company.

Lobato, D.J. (1993). Issues and interventions for young siblings of children with medical and developmental problems. In Z.

Stoneman & P.W. Berman (Eds.), *The effects of mental retardation, disability, and illness on sibling relationships*, (pp.85-95). Baltimore, Maryland: Paul H. Brookes Publishing Company.

Lobato, D., Faust, D. & Spirito, A. (1988). Examining the effects of chronic disease and disability on children's sibling relationships. *Journal of Pediatric Psychology*, 13(3), 389-407.

Mandleco, B., Olsen, S.F., Dyches, T. & Marshall, E. (2003). The relationship between family and sibling functioning in families raising a child with a disability. *Journal of Family Nursing*, 9(4), 365-396.

Manitoba Education and Training. (1998). *Individual Education Planning: A Handbook for Developing and Implementing IEP's, Early to Senior Years.*

Manitoba Education and Training. (2001). *Special Needs Categorical Funding Process Update.*

Manitoba Education and Training. (2001). *Towards Inclusions: From Challenges to Possibilities: Planning for Behaviour.*

Massimilla, E. (1956). *Heaven's Very Special Child.* Hatboro, PA: This is Our Life Publishing. This Is Our Life Publications, Box 21, Hatboro, PA 19040 USA

Meyer, D. & Vadasy, P. (1996). *Living with a brother or sister with special needs: A book for sibs* (2nd ed.). Seattle & London: University Washington Press.

Minot State University (1993-1997) Kimberley Leslie Smith's Undergraduate Class Notes.

National Association of Sibling Programs. *NASP Newsletter.* Winter 1993, Number 3.

Opperman, S. & Alant, E. (2003). The coping responses of the adolescent siblings of children with severe disabilities. *Disability and rehabilitation,* 25(9), 441.

Platt, A.J. (Personal communication about wills for people with disabilities, June 2004).

Powell, T.H. & Gallagher, P.A. (1993). *Brother's and sisters: A special part of exceptional families (2nd edition).* Baltimore: Paul H. Brookes Publishing Co.

Schubert, D.T. (n.d.). *Opportunities available to brothers and sisters.* Retrieved February 25, 2004, from http://www.autism.org/siblings/opportun.html

Schubert, D.T. (n.d.) *Sibling Needs: Helpful information for parents.* Retrieved February 24, 2004, from http://www.autism.org/sibling/sibneeds.html

Seltzer, M.M. & Krauss, M.W. (1993). Adult sibling relationships of persons with mental retardation. In Z. Stoneman & P.W. Berman (Eds.), *The effects of mental retardation, disability, and illness on sibling relationships,* (pp.99-113). Baltimore, Maryland: Paul H. Brookes Publishing Company.

Simeonsson, R. J. & McHale, S.M. (1981). Research on handicapped children: sibling relationships. *Child: Care, health and development,* 7, 153-171.

Singers, G.H.S., & Powers, L.E. (1993). *Families, disabilities, and empowerment: Active coping skills and strategies for family interventions.* Baltimore, Maryland: Paul H. Brookes Publishing Co.

Snell, M.E. (1993). *Instruction of students with severe disabilities* (4th ed.). New York, New York: Macmillan Publishing Company.

Society for Manitobans with Disabilities. (2002). *SMD and ME.*

Stoneman, Z. & Berman, P.W. (1993). *The effects of mental retardation, disability and illness on sibling relationships: Research issues and challenges.* Baltimore, Maryland: Paul H. Brookes Publishing Co.

Stoneman, Z. & Brody, G.H. (1993). Sibling relations in the family context. In Z.

Stoneman & P.W. Berman (Eds.), *The effects of mental retardation, disability and illness on sibling relationships,* (pp.3-26). Baltimore, Maryland: Paul H. Brookes Publishing Company.

Summers, M., Bridge, J. & Summers, C.R. (1991). Sibling Support Groups. *Teaching Exceptional Children,* 23(4), 20-25.

Thomas, G.E. (1996). *Teaching students with mental retardation: A life goal curriculum planning approach.* Englewood Cliffs, New Jersey: Prentice-Hall, Inc.

Turnball, A.P., & Turnball, H.R. (1997). *Families, professionals, and exceptionality: A special partnership.* Upper Saddle River, New Jersey: Prentice-Hall, Inc.

Valdiviesco, C., Ripley, S. & Ambler, L. (1988). Children with disabilities: Understanding sibling issues. *NICHY News Digest,* (11) Washington, D.C.: Interstate Research Associates.

Walmsley, D. (personal communication about Children's Special Services, June 2002)

Printed in the United States
61232LVS00003B/1-51